BOOKS BY KATHARINE MORRISON MC CLINTON

Handbook of Popular Antiques

Collecting American Glass

Complete Book of Small Antiques Collecting

Complete Book of Small Country Antiques

Antiques of American Childhood

Collecting American Victorian Antiques

Collecting American Nineteenth Century Silver

Antiques in Miniature

Antique Collecting for Everyone

ANTIQUES IN MINIATURE

Miniature China, all less than 3 inches high. *(Collection of Suzanne Stocking Mottahedeh)*

ANTIQUES IN MINIATURE

Katharine Morrison Mc Clinton

CHARLES SCRIBNER'S SONS / New York

1 3 5 7 9 11 13 15 17 19 M/P 20 18 16 14 12 10 8 6 4 2

Printed in the United States of America

Library of Congress Catalog Card Number 75-123843

ISBN 0-684-14540-5

ACKNOWLEDGMENTS

It is a pleasure to acknowledge the generous assistance of those who have aided me in gathering information and have given me the benefit of their advice. I wish especially to express my gratitude to Mr. Ivan M. Quimby, Registrar, Winterthur Museum, Winterthur, Delaware; Otto M. Wasserman, New York City; Mrs. Mildred Mottahedeh, Mottahedeh Inc., New York City; The Folger Coffee Company; Maude Feld; Philip Hammerslough; the Decorative Arts Department of The Henry Ford Museum. I also wish to thank the various dealers who have furnished photographs.

I owe a special thank you to my editor, Elinor Parker, for her interest and careful reading and editing of the manuscript of this my third book for Scribners. Also a thank you to my granddaughter Catharine Rule Ashley for typing the manuscript.

NOTE

Dimensions are given for nearly every piece; it has been impossible to reproduce the pictures in exact proportion to each other.

CONTENTS

ANTIQUES IN MINIATURE

Introduction

THE MAGIC OF THE TINY OR MINIATURE OBJECT HAS FASCINATED collectors in every period of history. With some it is the nostalgic sentimental appeal related to their childhood; with others it is the attraction of small things and the fact that they can be exhibited in little space such as bookcases, corner cupboards and mantel shelves. Whatever it is that makes one turn his collecting interest to miniatures, there are a vast number of collectors of miniature articles and the tiny objects are so varied that almost every category of antique collecting can also be pursued in miniature.

Artists and craftsmen themselves have always been interested in making tiny objects, from the glassblower who formed the "end-of-the-day" bit of glass into a toy to take home, to the famous goldsmith Fabergé, who turned his skill and artistry to designing miniatures of flowers in a vase. The publisher printed miniature books. Indeed, the making of tiny books antedates the beginning of printing, for there are small manuscript Books of Hours from the thirteenth and fourteenth centuries. Other workmen employed their skills in writing The Lord's Prayer on a pin head. All of these objects were first made for the amusement and diversion of the maker and later enjoyed by the collector.

Early miniatures were called toys. In the seventeenth and eighteenth centuries the toy was not a plaything for children but instead it was a small, dainty, delicate and often costly trinket for the amusement and diversion of the adult. Chelsea seals and toys are costly baubles. There are fine antiques made in miniature. This book is about this type of toy or miniature. Although it is not possible to treat some miniatures without the mention of dolls' house miniatures, generally speaking this book is about miniatures of a larger size and on a higher level of workmanship than that of the majority of dolls' house miniatures.

Miniatures are of three sizes. The smallest miniatures are those made for dolls' houses. The second size miniatures are those made for larger dolls or for cabinets, and the third size miniatures

Watercolor of a little girl and her toys, c. 1830. The stenciled armchair with pierced eagle-shaped splat is child's size. The group of doll's furniture in the foreground is late Sheraton style. This interesting picture illustrates two sizes of miniature. *(Courtesy John Gordon)*

are for the use of children themselves. This book is essentially about the second size miniature. It is about the rare and expensive miniature.

The craze for tiny objects and anything miniature goes back to the sixteenth and seventeenth centuries, when small objects of silver, china, glass, pewter and other materials, together with miniature furniture, were collected and displayed in cabinets. The Dutch arranged these treasures in bow-fronted cabinets with glass doors which were set on stands or hung on the wall. The costly miniatures on the shelves were for the amusement of the adult. These tiny baubles not only satisfied the love of beautiful materials and craftsmanship but also had a special appeal because they were small in scale and were often exact reproductions of the owner's household furnishings. Having such a cabinet was a fashionable hobby in the seventeenth century and those who could afford it indulged themselves in costly and magnificent miniature objects.

The vogue for making collections of tiny objects in cabinets was also popular in Germany. Here, in addition to cabinets, miniatures were assembled in a "Puppenhaus" as early as the 16th century. The famous Figdor Collection of miniature furniture, faïence and other tiny objects, some dating as early as 1568, is an example of collecting in miniature. The early "Puppenhaus", including many in the Germanisches Museum in Nüremberg, were to be seen, admired and to instruct but not to be played with. Such a cabinet as one dated 1639 accurately reproduces the decorative arts of the period in miniature from drawing room to cellar wine kegs and gives a picture of the life of the times.

In Italy the production of miniature objects was undoubtedly increased by the need for their use in the settings of crèche scenes which flourished, especially in Naples, from the Middle Ages on. Such scenes as the "Marriage Feast at Cana" included not only figures but also miniature dishes of pewter and glassware. The vogue for miniatures continued in Germany, Holland and Continental Europe through the eighteenth century.

In France the room rather than a house or cabinet was the

German and Dutch miniature chairs from the Figdor Collection. 16th Century.

popular type. But this was not for reasons of economy, for these rooms were so elaborate and so richly decorated that they cost as much as a whole house. In the mid-seventeenth century Madame de Maintenon had a miniature room. Cardinal Richelieu gave a miniature room to Princesse d'Enghien and a room was also given to the Duc de Maine. These rooms were to look at and to be toyed with but not to be disassembled and played with.

Although the cabinets and rooms were at first designed as a hobby for adults, the craze for making collections stimulated the toy industry and rooms with tiny objects also began to be made solely for the enjoyment of children. Nüremberg, Augsburg and Ulm became centers for making toys and miniatures.

That many costly miniatures were given to the children of the wealthy is evidenced by the existence of the dolls' house which was given by Queen Anne to her godchild Ann Sharp in c. 1700. It is filled with costly miniatures. These must have been made to look at and not to be played with. Indeed, the contents of the early cabinets, rooms and houses with their expensive miniatures were for royalty and the wealthy class and such toys were usually made to order. But even when these miniatures were given to children they were for wonder and visual enjoyment and not to be taken out and handled.

When the craze for collecting miniatures spread to England the English enlarged the idea and displayed their miniatures in houses. These were often models of their own houses and the exterior as well as the interior was reproduced in miniature. Sometimes they were designed and constructed by the same architect who designed the large house. The most famous example of this is the Nostell Priory dolls' house which was designed in 1735 by Robert

Miniature furniture from the Figdor Collection, Ulm, Germany, 16th Century. ABOVE: Two upholstered armchairs, c. 5 inches. BELOW: Closed-in bed with carving, 8 inches by 7¼ inches.

Miniature furniture from the Figdor Collection. Doll's carved cupboard, dated 1568. Walnut with intarsia of pine, pear, apple and maple. Family coat-of-arms on open doors. Size c. 8 inches by 7¼ inches. Miniature German pottery on shelves.

Adam. The furniture is attributed to Chippendale who was then an apprentice. Another well-known English dolls' house was attached to a stand in the manner of the Dutch cabinets. It was built in 1705 for the daughter of John Westbrook.

Adam, Sheraton and Chippendale were all involved in making dolls' houses at one time or another. The furnishings of these elegant and charming dolls' houses are among the great achievements of the English eighteenth century miniature maker. Each object was made by a craftsman of skill and the materials as well as the workmanship of these early miniatures is usually of the highest quality. Each class of objects was made by an expert in the field. Thus miniature pewter was made by a pewterer, silver by a silversmith, and pottery and porcelains at the factories where the larger articles were made. Of course, there are some articles of a provincial nature that do not display as fine workmanship but they have a certain naïve charm. While the miniature made by a fine cabinetmaker has more intrinsic worth, that made by a country carpenter or even an amateur has social and historic interest.

If you decide to collect antiques in miniature be sure that you can afford the luxury, for small things are not to be acquired at a small price. Miniatures are expensive, rare and not always available. Information about miniature antiques is also not easily found since most books ignore the miniature or give it only casual mention. However, antique dealers have become interested in miniatures and there are now tiny miniature chests, and pottery and porcelain miniatures to be found in the better shops. There are also reproductions in the market so the collector must beware not only of the marks, but of the quality, which is the final criterion of value.

Contrary to general belief, miniature silver is not always of fine workmanship. Some miniature porcelain and pottery is marked but many articles are not marked and we can only judge its worth by our own taste and appreciation of good design, color and workmanship.

Furniture

MOST PIECES OF MINIATURE FURNITURE OF FINE CRAFTSMANSHIP AND good enough to be considered along with larger furniture masterpieces were made after the middle of the seventeenth century when the furniture maker received the status of cabinetmaker. There were many small pieces made as samples or show pieces from which orders could be taken for larger pieces of similar design. The cabinetmaker's sample could have been made by the cabinetmaker himself or by an apprentice. These tiny pieces were used as travelling salesmen's samples or were displayed in the shop window. Many pieces of miniature furniture were also made to display valuable trinkets of silver or porcelain or to hold them in the miniature drawers. These pieces often sat upon the top of chests of drawers of matching design. The miniature furniture which corresponded in design to the larger pieces of furniture of the period was usually of fine quality. Still other pieces were country-made by a local carpenter. Many of these country pieces are also of good quality. Another class of miniature furniture was made by amateurs, perhaps by the man of the house. Miniature furniture was made in several sizes. Miniature furniture of the class with which we are concerned here ranges from five inches to thirty or forty inches in height for such pieces as a secretary, a chest-on-chest or highboy.

Miniature furniture was made in every style from Renaissance to late Victorian. There are miniature chests, cupboards, tables, buffets, dressers, chests of drawers, stools, chairs, beds, highboys, lowboys and looking glasses.

The earliest pieces of miniature furniture were in the Renaissance style and these were made of oak in Germany and Holland in the sixteenth and seventeenth centuries. There were heavy cupboards or shranks, with doors and drawers beneath. These were of architectural construction with heavy moldings and bun feet and ornamented with geometric carving and metal locks. Other pieces were inlaid with intarsia of pine, pear, apple and maple. Chairs were of several types, including armchairs with slipper feet and Italian-type folding chairs, as well as a simple German ladder-back type. Tables were both rectangular and circular with flap leaves. Early beds were of two types: the enclosed wall beds decorated with simple cut-work carving and turned poster beds with wooden testers or canopies. One seldom finds any of these early oak miniatures. However, some oak miniature furniture was made in England in the seventeenth century.

English Renaissance miniature furniture was carved with such motifs as the guilloche and acanthus leaf and strapwork designs. The articles of furniture included chests with straight short legs or bun feet, trestle tables and draw tables with heavy bulbous legs and straight stretchers close to the floor. Cupboards included almeries or hanging cupboards, court cupboards, credences and hutches. Beds had heavy carved wooden posts and a carved wooden canopy. There were benches and stools of simple construction, but few chairs. These were of two types, the high-backed chair with closed-in arms and the "X" or Italian type chair. There were also rocking and straight-legged pottie chairs for children. Cradles were of paneled oak and were made both with and without hoods. Miniature high chairs had solid carved backs, open arms and tall turned legs resting on stretchers close to the floor. The earliest ones did not have a step for the feet. These were usually sturdy country pieces. The majority of these were made in England in the eighteenth century but a few were made in America. English miniature furniture was also made in walnut, ash, yew, elm, and chestnut with inlays of holly and bogwood. The late seventeenth and eighteenth century pieces were made of walnut and mahogany.

Jacobean style miniature furniture was also made of oak, but the pieces were not as heavy as the earlier oak furniture. With the

Jacobean period English and American styles converge. Of course there are differences, but for the purposes of miniature furniture collectors general characteristics of the style will suffice and these are the same in both countries. Table and chair legs were turned. There were refectory tables, long and narrow, with bulbous turned legs, and gateleg tables with slender turned legs. Chairs were of wainscot or panel-back type and side chairs had carved open backs with spindles connecting to an arched top rail. Later, in the Restoration or Charles II period, chairs were elaborately carved and had caned backs and seats. There were also benches and stools, love seats and daybeds with carving and cane-work. Beds were of poster style, panelled, carved, and draped with curtains. Chests, hanging cupboards, court cupboards, buffets and dressers all continued in use. The oak furniture was often inlaid. These pieces may be seen in museums but such miniature furniture is not on the market.

The earliest antique miniature furniture that one would be likely to find in shops today is that made of walnut and belonging to the styles of William and Mary and Queen Anne. William and Mary chairs had high backs with a carved crest and carved scroll or trumpet-shaped legs or spirally turned legs with carved or lyre-shaped stretchers. Chests of drawers, lowboys, and highboys of Dutch influence had beautiful designs of marquetry or lacquer work. Tall-case clocks and mirrors were similarly decorated. A late seventeenth century miniature William and Mary writing table is in the Victoria & Albert Museum and a Queen Anne drop-leaf table of walnut with cabriole legs is also in the collection of the Victoria & Albert Museum. Windsor chairs of various types were also made at this time, and there were chests, desks and highboys made of walnut. These pieces were often inlaid with boxwood and other light woods or ivory or bone, and some pieces are found with ivory knobs or original brasses and escutcheons. Such sophisticated pieces were made by cabinet-makers. Some miniatures of this type were made in America after the mid-eighteenth century.

The walnut furniture of the Queen Anne period is simple with little carving except for a shell or some other simple design on the knees of legs. The furniture is squatty and comfortable. Chairs have rounding backs with a center vase-shaped splat and cabriole legs. There were love seats, daybeds, chairs, highboys, lowboys, card tables, gateleg tables, tripod tables and game tables. Lacquer and inlay decoration was still used, and beautiful damasks, velvets and especially needlework were used for upholstery.

Of course, not all of these pieces were made in miniature, but such pieces as highboys, lowboys, chairs, tables, and tall clocks of the Queen Anne period have been found in miniature both in England and America.

Miniature highboy and tall clock. American 1731. Carved and painted red and gold. *(Philadelphia Museum of Art)*

Miniature mahogany Chippendale ladder-back chairs, carved ribbon-backed chairs and splat-backed Chippendale chairs with cabriole legs and claw and ball feet were also made in miniature. To be sure, not many of these pieces exist today, but there are enough to make the search worthwhile for the serious, patient collector.

There were also miniature chairs, tables, beds, desks, secretaries, breakfront bookcases, sideboards and other articles of Hepplewhite design. Hepplewhite chairs had shield-shaped backs and were made of mahogany or satinwood. They were carved and sometimes inlaid with fruitwoods. Beds had four fluted posts and a curved molding for a canopy which formed a frame for a valance of chintz. Sheraton furniture was classic in design and the chairs had straight legs, sometimes turned or fluted, and straight backs with vertical or horizontal splats. The fancy chair and the Windsor chair were also popular at this time. Dining tables were rectangular and narrow with tripod leg supports. There were also small circular tripod tables and drum tables, sideboards, side tables, knife cases and wine coolers. In America, Duncan Phyfe furniture was an outgrowth of the Sheraton style, and while we have no record that Phyfe made miniature furniture it seems very probable that he may have made dolls' furniture for the child of some well-known person and it is even possible that such may come to light some day.

When we come to the Empire period, miniature furniture had begun to be manufactured in great quantity and was no longer the work of an individual craftsman. There were Empire chairs showing Grecian influence, heavy pedestal tables, sleigh beds, bureaus, secretaries, and many other articles. These pieces are all available in miniature today and are found in both walnut and better finished mahogany.

The Victorian era was the heyday of the dolls' house and it lasted from the 1840's to 1900. During this time various styles of furniture were made for the dolls' use, from carved rosewood to walnut and golden oak and even iron. There was furniture with French influence and furniture of Gothic influence and finally tufted upholstered pieces that had no wood showing at all. When iron furniture became popular miniature iron chairs were made with Gothic fretwork backs.

Furniture styles influenced the use of certain woods. The simple sturdy pieces of furniture were made of oak for strength. For economy, the parts that didn't show were made of inexpensive woods as was the furniture which was to be painted. Also, the woods available in the region where the furniture was made determined the wood most used.

Dutch miniature furniture reflects the styles of France, Germany and England. In the early cabinets there are high-backed chairs and tables with twisted Flemish legs connected by low stretchers. Miniature cabinets also have William and Mary trumpet legs connected by X stretchers. Other cabinets have exaggerated Baroque bulges and curved panels and tops. These Baroque style pieces are the ones that are available to collectors today. There are Dutch chests of drawers with bombé fronts in Baroque style measuring 12½ inches in height, 14½ inches in length and 10 inches in depth. There are also Indo-Dutch miniature chests made in the eighteenth century of pine, walnut and padouk. The shapes are Baroque style and the little pieces have a heavy appearance. An Indo-Dutch eighteenth century Georgian padouk miniature desk set on heavy bun feet measures 27½ inches in height. There are also eighteenth century bureau-cabinets or secretaries with molded cornice and broken pediments measuring 24 inches in height. Serpentine-front chests of drawers are sometimes decorated with découpage of chinoiserie in Rococo cartouches on a black ground.

The "Cabinet of Art Curios" in the Gemeentemuseum in The Hague dates from the year 1760, and the William and Mary style furniture, partly Dutch and partly English, is made of walnut.

French miniature furniture was made in all styles from Louis XIII to Directoire. Miniature oak buffets were made in Louis XIII style, and French miniature antique rooms in Louis XVI, Empire and Directoire style were exhibited at the Exposition Universelle de Paris in 1900. Also exhibited was a hanging miniature kitchen

ABOVE: Louis XV serpentine inlaid walnut commode banded with light wood inlay. Height 7¼ inches; width 11 inches. LOWER LEFT: French Directoire acajou commode with brass mountings, peg feet. Height 12 inches. LOWER RIGHT: Louis XVI kingwood commode banded and inlaid. Height 13 inches; width 13¾ inches. *(Taylor & Dull photo)*

with pots, pans and doll cooks, set within a framework of Rococo bronze doré. This was the work of the great Caffieri whose work also decorated Louis XV commodes. The French fascination for miniatures supported several eighteenth century miniature makers. Biennais was a French toy cabinetmaker in the eighteenth and nineteenth centuries, and Lobjoy also specialized in miniature furniture at the establishment on rue Saint-Antoine in Paris in the early nineteenth century. Miniature chests in Louis XV and Louis XVI styles were similar to the large-sized chests. The Louis XV chests had ornate Rococo metal decorations and drawer pulls. The legs were curved as was the body structure. Louis XVI chests had fluted decoration on drawers and body. Both Louis XV and Louis XVI chests were made of mahogany and fruitwoods, and some have elaborate inlay. They usually have marble tops.

The French miniature furniture available today is generally of Louis XV, Louis XVI and Directoire styles. The pieces are made of walnut and inlaid with tulip, holly, sycamore and other colored woods. The inlays consist of borders and simple patterns such as stars and checks. The ormolu metal mounts are similar in design to those on larger pieces. A few pieces of eighteenth century French miniature furniture were in a Parke-Bernet sale of May 5, 1939. They were described as follows: "Louis XV inlaid walnut commode, serpentine front banded with light wood inlay, 7½ inches by 11 inches," "Directoire brass mounted acajou commode, rectangular

LEFT: Serpentine front walnut commode with shaped feet. Height 19½ inches; width 19½ inches. Provincial 18th Century type. RIGHT: Walnut Louis XV settee with leaf and shell carving, tapestry upholstery. Length 35 inches. French 18th Century. (*Taylor & Dull photo*)

brass moldings and bands, peg feet, 12 inches by 12 inches." "Louis XVI inlaid kingwood banded and inlaid. 13 inches by 13¾ inches." "Louis XVI inlaid chiffonier with white marble top measures 16½ inches by 10¾ inches." "Charles X acajou dining table, oval top, hinged leaves, square tapered legs. 6½ inches by 16 inches. c. 1825." An eighteenth century antique French miniature serpentine front commode and a Louis XV settee with shell and leaf carving were in a sale of January 22, 1943. A carved fruitwood Directoire miniature bedstead made in the late eighteenth century is 21 inches long. It has shaped and molded head and foot panels and turned peg feet.

There are also miniatures in French Provincial style. Chests of drawers and open cupboards and tables have simple flower and leaf carvings and are made of fruitwood. French miniature furniture was made for dolls and children, but the majority of the pieces of fine French miniature were made by the cabinetmaker as show pieces from which orders were taken for larger pieces. It was also

Miniature chair. France, 18th Century. Miniature Louis XVI chest of drawers, mahogany with gouge carving. French, 18th Century. *(Cooper Union Museum for the Arts of Decoration)*

the style to display tiny miniature pieces in glass cabinets together with other trinkets.

CHESTS OF DRAWERS

THE most available piece of miniature furniture was the chest of drawers. Every type from early eighteenth century oak chests-on-stands to Empire mahogany bureaus of the 1840's and 1850's were made in fairly large quantities, to judge from the number available today. Indeed so many are on the market that it seems evident that they are not all cabinetmaker's show pieces nor are they dolls' furniture, but some pieces must have been made by popular demand for use on a dressing table or large chest to hold jewelry, handkerchiefs, gloves and other small articles. Many of these little chests that do not relate to any definite furniture style can certainly be put in this category. One such chest, 14 inches high by 4½ inches deep, is fitted with tea boxes, a mirror, a sewing drawer and a writing compartment.

Early oak chests are rare and those of walnut are almost as rare. A rare American paneled oak chest 1670-1700 measures 14⅞ inches x 12½ inches x 20 inches. It is illustrated in Wallace Nutting's *"Furniture Treasury,"* as is an oak chest with ball feet and double arch molding. (1700-1710.) Similar pine chests with ball feet and tear-drop handles have from one to three drawers. These may have been made as separate pieces of furniture or were intended to stand on top of larger chests to hold small articles.

English oak chests with gouged geometric carving and ball feet date from the seventeenth century. These are very rare. William and Mary style chests of drawers were made in walnut and were often veneered in satinwood, ebony or burl walnut in herringbone pattern and some chests have ivory inlay and ivory knobs on the drawers. Chippendale chests of drawers were made of mahogany in the late eighteenth century and some were also made of deal and yew, cherry, ash and elm. Sheraton and Hepplewhite chests were

Connecticut block-front chest, cherry or mahogany, c. 1755. Doll's size. *(Index of American Design)*

LEFT: American curly maple chest ot drawers, Chippendale style. Height 20¼ inches.
BELOW: Top of chest with date, 1764, gouged in the wood. *(Both courtesy Philip H. Bradley)*

also made of mahogany. Many of these chests had string inlay of contrasting wood such as applewood, holly, or bogwood and had ivory knobs and key plates. From 1790 to 1850 there are mahogany chests of drawers in the various styles from Chippendale, Sheraton and Hepplewhite to Federal and Empire.

There are also certain local differences which are evident in the miniatures, such as the unique chest in Connecticut block-front style made c. 1755. It has its original brasses and the wood is cherry or mahogany. A rare curly maple Chippendale chest is marked on top, 1764. Curly maple chests were also made in Sheraton style.

American miniature chest of drawers with shaped apron, bracket feet and molded top edge. 10¼ inches long, 12 inches high, 6 inches deep. *(Courtesy Ginsburg & Levy, Inc.)*

Miniature chest with ball feet, poplar wood painted red. New England, c. 1710. *(Courtesy Wadsworth Atheneum, Hartford)*

ABOVE LEFT: Miniature chest of drawers, mahogany, American, 1790-1800. Drawers outlined in brown-stained inlay bands. Brass drawer knobs, scalloped skirt, French feet. 15½ inches high; 17⅞ inches wide; 8¾ inches deep. (*Courtesy Henry Francis du Pont Winterthur Museum*)

RIGHT: Child's chest of drawers. Mahogany, New England, c. 1790. Serpentine front, bracket feet, oval brasses, bail handles. 25⅝ inches high, 25⅞ inches wide, 10½ inches deep. (*Courtesy Henry Francis du Pont Winterthur Museum*)

Important miniature chest of drawers. Mahogany with satinwood panel decorated with inlay. Hepplewhite style with shaped apron, French splayed feet. 17 inches high, 18½ inches wide, 10 inches deep. Signed under bottom drawer, "William Lloyde, Springfield, Massachusettes, February 16, 1807." (*Courtesy The Henry Ford Museum, Dearborn, Michigan*)

LEFT: Pennsylvania miniature chest, three drawers, bracket feet, natural wood finish. 10 inches high, 8¹⁵⁄₁₆ inches wide, 4⅝ inches deep. 1759-1800. *(Courtesy Henry Francis du Pont Winterthur Museum)*

BELOW LEFT: Chest of drawers, mahogany inlaid with band of tulip wood in diamond shapes. Chevron pattern at chamfered corners, French feet, carved bead moldings. 1790-1800. Middle States. 16 inches high, 15⅜ inches wide, 7¾ inches deep. *(Courtesy Henry Francis du Pont Winterthur Museum)*

RIGHT: Miniature chest of drawers, mahogany, American, c. 1815. Triple reeded front posts, circular brass pulls, cup-disk and compressed-ball-turned feet. 14⅝ inches high, 13⅜ inches wide, 7⅜ inches deep. *(Courtesy Henry Francis du Pont Winterthur Museum)*

Victorian style bureau. Height 8½ inches; width 8⅜ inches. Loring C. Cushing, South Hingham, Massachusetts, c. 1830-1850. *(Courtesy Old Ordinary, South Hingham, Massachusetts)*

RIGHT: Miniature blanket chest. Pine painted green with red outlines and red, yellow and black leaf decoration and initials "L.H." Pennsylvania, 1820-1840. 14¾ inches high, 9⅞ inches wide, 6½ inches deep. *(Courtesy Henry Francis du Pont Winterthur Museum)*

A great many pieces of miniature furniture were made in Pennsylvania. Some of these were of mahogany or curly maple and were of well-constructed sophisticated cabinetwork. Others were obviously made by a country cabinetmaker or an amateur. Many in these latter categories were of pine and were painted and sometimes marked with a name and date. The decoration was usually of leaves and flowers but a tiny chest in the New-York Historical Society Collection has a painted scene of a village with trees and houses.

Walnut bombé storage cabinet in Dolls' House. Height c. 7½ inches; width c. 4½ inches; depth c. 2 inches. 17th Century, Dutch. *(Collection Haags Gemeentemuseum, The Hague)*

COFFERS AND CHESTS-ON-STANDS OR HIGHBOYS

EARLY cupboards, storage chests and coffers are often found in Dutch and German miniatures. English chests-on-legs were made of oak in the early eighteenth century. Most American miniature coffers were of Pennsylvania origin and were related to the Pennsylvania Dutch dower chests. These date from the mid-eighteenth century down to about 1840. They were made of walnut, tulip, cherry and similar woods and were painted or inlaid with tulips or other Pennsylvania Dutch motifs and many also had a name and date. Some coffers had flat bases while others had scroll or ogee bracket feet or round bun feet. In size the chests ranged from 5½ inches to 15 inches in height. There were also tall oak kas and highboys of chest-on-

Footed walnut miniature chest with Chester County type inlay on front. Length 14½ inches; height 6⅛ inches; depth 8⅛ inches. Chester County, Pa., 1750. *(Courtesy Henry Francis du Pont Winterthur Museum)*

Miniature chest painted dark olive green, tan and black. Name and date, "Caterina Wittmeren, 1763" inscribed on front. Height 7¼ inches; width 16⅝ inches; depth 8½ inches. *(Courtesy Henry Francis du Pont Winterthur Museum)*

Highboy, William and Mary style, walnut inlaid with lighter wood, trumpet legs, curved X stretchers and scalloped apron. Height c. 8 inches; width c. 4 inches; depth c. 2 inches. Dutch. *(Collection Haags Gemeentemuseum, The Hague)*

Painted pine dower chest decorated with gray and vermilion tulips "M.S." and date, 1791. Length 23½ inches. *(Taylor & Dull photo)*

Miniature Pennsylvania dower chest with tulip pattern medallion, name and date inlaid in wax. "Johannes/17/73/Mosser." Iron hinges. Height 7⅜ inches; width 14⅞ inches; depth 8½ inches. *(Courtesy Henry Francis du Pont Winterthur Museum)*

Miniature teakwood chest-on-chest with double arched pediment and arched doors opening to shelves and small drawers. Brass escutcheons on outside, ogee bracket feet. England or West Indies, 1725-1750. Height 30¾ inches; width 21½ inches; depth 11½ inches. *(Courtesy Henry Francis du Pont Winterthur Museum)*

Chest on stand, mahogany, English c. 1790. Dentilled cornice surmounted by an unusually shaped top, ivory knobs. Height 16½ inches; width 7¼ inches; depth 5½ inches. *(Courtesy Rupert Gentle)*

Chippendale style oak kas. Height 28½ inches; width 21 inches. Pennsylvania, 18th Century. *(Taylor & Dull photo)*

American miniature walnut highboy with broken-arch pediment with carved rosettes; three ball and spike finials; cabriole legs, pad feet and double ball-drops at bottom. Carved fans on two drawers. Height 18 inches; width 10½ inches; depth 6⅛ inches. Connecticut, 1750-1780. *(Courtesy Henry Francis du Pont Winterthur Museum)*

chest form with doors and storage drawers beneath. In height they range from 28 inches to 30 inches. These chests-on-stands or high-boys are rare. Miniature American highboys were made in Queen Anne style with cabriole legs, in William and Mary style with trumpet legs and also in Chippendale style with bracket feet. They date from 1770 to 1790. These are illustrated in Wallace Nutting's *Furniture Treasury.* The highboy in the Essex Institute was made by an amateur in the late eighteenth century. It is 22 inches high, made of pine and painted to simulate graining and marbling. The majority of the miniature highboys are taller. Another highboy of elaborate design was made in Philadelphia c. 1760. It is constructed of mahogany, poplar and pine and has claw and ball feet with carved knees. A carved shell ornaments the apron and a bonnet top has pierced carving. This unique piece was undoubtedly made to display the work of the cabinetmaker.

LEFT: Miniature mahogany hanging corner cupboard. Height 29 inches. English, 18th Century. RIGHT: Miniature walnut cabinet. Height 15¾ inches. English, 17th Century. (*Courtesy Otto M. Wasserman*)

LOWBOYS OR DRESSING TABLES

MINIATURE lowboys or dressing tables were made in William and Mary, Queen Anne and Chippendale styles. They were generally made of mahogany. Those of William and Mary style have trumpet legs and x stretchers while the legs of Queen Anne and Chippendale style lowboys are cabriole with pad feet. Lowboys usually have one long and two short drawers. They measure from 7 to 9 inches in height. The majority of the miniature American lowboys were made in New England from the mid-eighteenth century to the first quarter of the nineteenth century. The lowboy is one of the most attractive pieces of miniature furniture. It is often of fine workmanship and good proportions and compares favorably with large-size pieces. Lowboys are rare and expensive.

Chippendale mahogany lowboy with robust cabriole legs and valanced skirt. Height 9 inches. Philadelphia, 18th Century. *(Taylor & Dull, photo)*

Miniature dressing table, mahogany and pine with cabriole legs and pad feet and shell-carved center drawer. Height 9 inches; width 11⅞ inches; depth 7⅝ inches. New England, 1725-1750. *(Courtesy Henry Francis du Pont Winterthur Museum)*

Miniature lowboy, maple and walnut with slim cabriole legs, pad feet. Height 15½ inches; width 20¾ inches, depth 11½ inches. Massachusetts, 1740-1760. *(Courtesy Henry Francis du Pont Winterthur Museum)*

DESKS AND SECRETARIES

EARLY miniature desks were of pine or curly maple. There are miniature desks of several different types. Miniature slant-top desks range

LEFT: Miniature bookcase-secretary. Rosewood and satinwood. Height 28 inches. English, c. 1760. *(Courtesy Otto M. Wasserman)*

CENTER: Miniature walnut secretary with broken pediment and shaped skirt with French feet. Height 15¾ inches. English, early 18th Century. *(Courtesy Otto M. Wasserman)*

RIGHT: Miniature bookcase, with crude pediment top, Gothic arch windows and serpentine base. Height 26 inches. English, 19th Century. *(Courtesy Otto M. Wasserman)*

in size from 8 inches to 30 inches in height. William and Mary style slant-top desks with bulbous or short turned legs were made in America in the late eighteenth century of both walnut and maple. Some desks had wooden drawer knobs and others were fitted with fine hardware of the period. Similar desks were made with Chippendale bracket feet. One of the finest pieces of miniature furniture in the Winterthur Museum is a cylinder-fall desk of high style which is attributed to a Maryland or Pennsylvania cabinetmaker. It is made of walnut with light and dark wood inlays of shell and seawood forms and patterns of stringing. The desk measures 16½ inches in

LEFT: Late Georgian pearwood miniature dresser with broken pediment. Height 18 inches; width 10 inches. CENTER: Georgian mahogany miniature secretary. Height 22 inches; width 10 inches. English, 18th Century. RIGHT: Georgian miniature mahogany cabinet-bookcase with broken pediment. Height 18 inches. English, early 19th Century. *(Taylor & Dull photo)*

Miniature American slant-top desk with bracket feet, brass knobs and escutcheons on drawers. Pine, painted dark brown; interior dull brick red. Label on base: "New Toy Shop/ in Arch-Street, three doors below Fifth-Street,/ Philadelphia./ A handsome assortment of English and German Toys just opened and for sale, Wholesale and/ Retail, cheap for Cash or a short Credit./ Abraham Forst/ July 4, 1816." *(Courtesy Henry Francis du Pont Winterthur Museum)*

Child's desk on frame. Cherry, cabriole legs, pad feet, serpentine skirt. American, 1750-1800. Height 34⅛ inches; width 22¾ inches; depth (open) 19⅛ inches. *(Courtesy Henry Francis du Pont Winterthur Museum)*

Rare miniature American secretary with broken pediment. Walnut with mahogany ball finials inlaid in maple. Secondary woods, poplar and pine. Serpentine base with French feet. Height 49½ inches. Pennsylvania, c. 1790. *(Courtesy The Henry Ford Museum, Dearborn, Michigan)*

Miniature bombé desk with shaped and carved apron. Height 25½ inches; width 24 inches. Indo-Dutch, mid-18th Century. *(Taylor & Dull photo)*

Miniature desk. Chippendale, walnut and mahogany. Height 19½ inches; width 17 inches; depth 12 inches. English, c. 1790. *(Courtesy Marie Whitney)*

Miniature Georgian secretary. Broken pediment top, bracket feet. Height 24 inches; width 12½ inches. *(Taylor & Dull photo)*

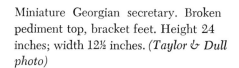

Miniature roll-top desk with curved skirt and French feet. American walnut and pine inlaid with shell motif in veneered cylinder front and string inlay around drawers and body. Height, 16½ inches; width 15 inches; depth 8 inches. American, c. 1790. *(Courtesy Henry Francis du Pont Winterthur Museum)*

William and Mary miniature walnut slant-top desk with short turned legs. Height 10½ inches; width 10 inches. American, 18th Century. *(Taylor & Dull photo)*

height. A scalloped apron connects the delicate feet and there are ring brasses. There were also miniature knee-hole desks and desk bookcases or secretaries. A secretary in the Henry Ford Museum measures 49½ inches in height. It is of Hepplewhite style made of walnut and has mahogany finials inlaid with maple. It was made c. 1790–1800 and probably in Pennsylvania.

Miniature fall-front desk. Height 9¼ inches; width 7½ inches; depth 4½ inches. Loring Cushing, 1830-1850. *(Courtesy Old Ordinary, Hingham, Massachusetts)*

Child's desk. Maple, American, c. 1750. Height 26½ inches; width 20 inches. *(Courtesy Ginsburg & Levy, Inc.)*

DRESSERS AND SIDEBOARDS

MINIATURE dressers were made to display the tiny pieces of pewter and china. These dressers were made both in Europe and America. Those made in the nineteenth century are the most available today. These are comparatively large, measuring from twelve to fifteen

Miniature sideboard, mahogany with line inlay, patera on legs. Height 16⅝ inches; width 22⅝ inches ;depth 19⅝ inches. New England, c. 1780. *(Courtesy Henry Francis du Pont Winterthur Museum)*

Miniature sideboard, Sheraton style, mahogany with inlaid double heart on top, line inlay on front panels and legs. Original oval brasses. Height 13⅞ inches; width 20⅞ inches; depth 9 inches. Massachusetts, 1790-1810. *(Courtesy Henry Francis du Pont Winterthur Museum)*

Miniature sample sideboard. Mahogany with inlay, turned feet, circular brasses. New York State. Signed on bottom of drawers: "December 24, 1823. Made by J. Curtis." Height 10⅞ inches; width 18⅞ inches; depth 4½ inches. *(Courtesy Henry Francis du Pont Winterthur Museum)*

Miniature painted pine dresser with scalloped apron. Height 21½ inches; width 15½ inches; depth 6¼ inches. American, 19th Century. Miniature pewter on shelves, European. *(Courtesy of the New-York Historical Society, New York City)*

inches in height and are made of woods such as hickory and elm and some pieces are painted. The majority of the miniature sideboards are made of mahogany and are of Sheraton or Hepplewhite style. They were made in both England and America but judging from the few seen today they were scarce when made and many times scarcer and rarer today. They are usually cabinetmakers' samples.

The few American miniature sideboards were made in New England, New York and Pennsylvania. They date from the late eighteenth century until the first quarter of the nineteenth century. A mahogany breakfront sideboard in the Winterthur Museum was made in Massachusetts between 1790 and 1810. It stands 13⅞ inches high and has a double heart inlay on top and a line inlay decorates the front panels and drawers. It has the original oval brasses. This beautifully constructed piece is of Sheraton style.

A mahogany sideboard with inlay of various types along the top edges of the drawers and a diamond shape in the center drawer was made in New York State and marked, "December 24, 1823 made by J. Curtis." James Curtis was a cabinetmaker so that this piece could have been made as a display sample of his work. The piece is 10⅜ inches high; 18⅞ inches long; and 4½ inches in depth. Another cabinetmaker's sideboard is of a little later date and is Empire style with spiral columns. It is of mahogany cross-banded at the sides and front and the top is hinged to show the construction. It measures 24 inches in height; 26 inches in length and 14½ inches in depth.

Miniature Empire serving table, mahogany with curly maple inlay, carving and marble top. Marked: "Made and Presented by F. T. Johnston Cabinet Maker/ No. 343 South Fort Below Almon/ March 29th, 1834." Height 9½ inches. (*Courtesy of The Henry Ford Museum, Dearborn, Michigan*)

TABLES

Miniature oak gateleg tables with turned legs were made in England in the seventeenth century. Queen Anne drop-leaf tables with cabriole legs were made in walnut in the eighteenth century. Al-

Hepplewhite dining table, 2 inches in height. Chairs, Hepplewhite, 3 inches in height. *(Courtesy of The Henry Ford Museum, Dearborn, Michigan)*

Sheraton mahogany two-part dining table with carved tripod supports. Height 3 inches. Chippendale ladder-back chairs. Height 5 inches. *(Courtesy of The Henry Ford Museum, Dearborn, Michigan)*

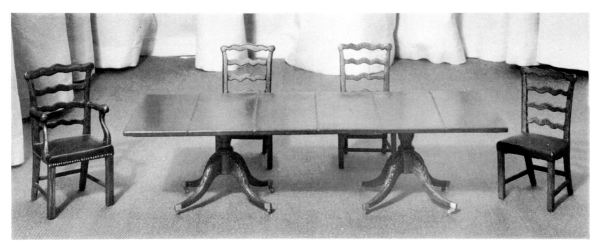

though the tables of this type were fine in workmanship they were usually small in size, thus any under five inches high may be considered dolls' house furniture. There were, however, tea tables and candlestands from ten to twelve inches in height. These were made of mahogany and cherry in the late eighteenth and early nineteenth centuries in America. They had a circular mahogany top with a turned shaft with urn and the tripod base terminated in snake feet. Similar tables were made in England. There were also small tables with square tops and a shaped skirt. The circular tapered legs terminated in pad feet. Small square tables with a drawer and turned

LEFT: Mahogany tripod table, square top and two drawers. Height c. 10 inches. American, c. 1800. *(Courtesy Henry Francis du Pont Winterthur Museum)*

CENTER: Miniature tea table. Mahogany top, cherry shaft with urn, tripod base with snake feet. Height 11 inches. American, 1800-1815. *(Courtesy Henry Francis du Pont Winterthur Museum)*

RIGHT: Miniature table, maple, mahogany and tulip. Square top with drawer, turned legs and tapered feet. Height 17½ inches. American, 1800-1820. *(Courtesy Henry Francis du Pont Winterthur Museum)*

Oak flap table with circular top 8½ inches in diameter. Queen Anne cabriole legs. English, 18th Century. *(Victoria & Albert Museum)*

legs with tapered feet were made in both maple and mahogany early in the nineteenth century. There were also kitchen work tables, Pembroke tables and refectory tables, but these were usually found in small size and in rough workmanship. A rare inlaid miniature chess table is in the collection of the New-York Historical Society. It is made of fruitwood and has delicate tapered legs and was probably made in France or Italy in the early nineteenth century.

CHAIRS

WINGED armchairs and commode chairs were the earliest type made in both England and America. There are many miniature chairs ranging from eight to fifteen inches in height. Smaller chairs were for dolls' houses and those of larger proportions were not miniatures but made for a child. Small oak settles are rarer than chairs. The majority of the chairs available to the collector are country type such as ladder-back and spindle-back chairs with rush seats. They are made of maple, ash and elm. Some are made of pine and stenciled and painted. Windsor armchairs of various types were painted

Miniature pine settle. Height 9½ inches. Loring Cushing, 1830-1850. *(Courtesy Old Ordinary, Hingham, Massachusetts)*

Miniature pine chair, Carver type, with three vertical and three horizontal spindles. Height 18¼ inches. American 18th Century. *(Index of American Design)*

Miniature child's chair, Brewster type. Hickory with slip-bottom seat, painted red. Height 23½ inches. Hickory washstand. Height c. 11 inches. American, 18th Century. *(Index of American Design)*

Miniature maple chair. Brewster type ladder-back with rush seat and turned legs ending in pad feet. Natural wood finish. Height 16⅝ inches. Upper Delaware Valley, c. 1780-1820. *(Courtesy Henry Francis du Pont Winterthur Museum)*

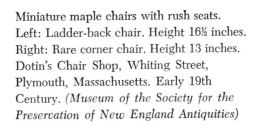

Miniature maple chairs with rush seats. Left: Ladder-back chair. Height 16½ inches. Right: Rare corner chair. Height 13 inches. Dotin's Chair Shop, Whiting Street, Plymouth, Massachusetts. Early 19th Century. *(Museum of the Society for the Preservation of New England Antiquities)*

LEFT: Miniature side chair with tapered legs, back with spindles and concave cresting rail. Painted red with yellow outlines and yellow and black flowers on crest rail. Height 8¹¹⁄₁₆ inches. New York or Pennsylvania, 1820-1840.

BELOW: Miniature settee painted red with black and gold decoration of squirrel, song book and trumpets, elaborately turned stiles and rails; legs and stretchers; scrolled arms. Pennsylvania, 1820-1840. Height 15¼ inches; width 24¾ inches. *(Both, courtesy Henry Francis du Pont Winterthur Museum)*

Miniature chair with vase-shaped splat, rush seat, tapered cylindrical legs on pad feet, turned stretchers. Maple, painted dark green with yellow leafy decoration. Height 16½ inches. Hudson River Valley, 1730-1750. *(Courtesy Henry Francis du Pont Winterthur Museum)*

black or green and date from the late eighteenth century. They were made in both England and America. There were also rare Windsor settees and spindle-back settees. Sheraton maple chairs with caned slats were made c. 1830. Stenciled parlor chairs with turned spindles date a few years later. There were also painted and stenciled Hitchcock side chairs with both solid and rush seats, and Boston rockers are also found in miniature. Walnut and mahogany chairs were made

RIGHT: Carved miniature mahogany Chippendale chair with cabriole legs and claw and ball feet. Height c. 6 inches. *(Courtesy The Henry Ford Museum, Dearborn, Michigan)*

BELOW: Rare miniature Chippendale mahogany settee with serpentine-shaped back, straight quadrangular legs. Length 30 inches. Philadelphia, 18th Century. *(Taylor & Dull photo)*

LEFT: Queen Anne walnut rush seat armchair with curved crest rail and vase splat, cabriole legs with pad feet. Height c. 12 inches. Pennsylvania, 18th Century. RIGHT: Rare Chippendale carved walnut chair, 18th Century, Pennsylvania. *(Taylor & Dull photo)*

in Queen Anne and Chippendale styles. These date from the late eighteenth century and are rare. In a sale of miniature furniture some ten years ago a fine carved walnut Chippendale chair and a serpentine-arched back mahogany Chippendale upholstered settee brought high prices while the majority of the other pieces which would now be considered desirable went for very low bids.

Bronze doll chairs. Height c. 7 inches. 1845. *(Museum of the City of New York)*

CRADLES AND BEDS

CRADLES of miniature sizes were made from the Middle Ages. The earliest cradles available to the collector were of oak and were hooded. These were made in England in the seventeenth century. They range in size from five inches to eighteen inches long. This simple type of rectangular cradle with hood, slanting sides and rocker feet continued to be made in mahogany, pine and fruitwoods through the nineteenth century. Sometimes there are elongated openings cut out for fingers and sometimes the cradle has turned posts and some cradles are painted and ornamented with flowers.

Beds were made with high hexagonal, octagonal or turned posts and headboards. Some posts and legs were baluster type and

Group of doll furniture. LEFT: Chest of drawers, Sheraton style. CENTER: Poster bed: RIGHT: Victorian chest of drawers. American, c. 1850. *(Essex Institute)*

Child's bed with turned posts and arched tester. Height 58½ inches; width 35½ inches. American, 1800-1815. *(Courtesy Henry Francis du Pont Winterthur Museum)*

Child's carved four-poster bed. New Jersey, 19th Century. *(Index of American Design)*

Doll's four-poster bed. American, late 18th Century. (*Museum of the City of New York*)

Doll's hooded cradle, pine. Length c. 27 inches. (*Museum of the City of New York*)

others were turned in block, vase, urn and ring pattern. The headboards were low and shaped and many beds have arched or flat canopies. A combination of woods was used, including pine and tulip. A few of these beds date from the late eighteenth century but the majority of them were made in the nineteenth century.

There were many small wooden accessories such as hanging shelves, footstools and boxes of various types but the majority of these articles were of dolls' house size and are of late manufacture.

MIRRORS

THE mirror or looking glass stands out in interest because it was related to the various types of furniture and reflected the period

LEFT: Miniature looking glass, Chippendale type. Scrolled top and bottom, reeded molding around glass. Height 8⅞ inches; width 5⅞ inches. Mahogany, American, 1800-1900. *(Courtesy Henry Francis du Pont Winterthur Museum)*

CENTER: Miniature looking glass, plain rectangular frame with a pierced arched tab at top for hanging. Height 5½ inches; width 3½ inches. Pine, New England, 1800-1830. *(Courtesy Henry Francis du Pont Winterthur Museum)*

RIGHT: Miniature looking glass. Rectangular with overhanging cornice. Frame gilded. Gilt and black basket of featherlike flowers on white ground painted in frieze panel. Height 5⁵⁄₁₆ inches; width 4¾ inches. English or American, 1810-1820. *(Courtesy Henry Francis du Pont Winterthur Museum)*

styles. Miniature looking glasses usually date from the late eighteenth century to 1850. In size they range from five inches to eleven inches in height.

A looking glass with scrolled outlines at top and bottom and outflaring ears at the corners was known as a Chippendale mirror. It was made of mahogany in large size from about 1800. Similar style looking glasses of mahogany were also made in miniature sizes. Plain rectangular looking glasses with a pierced arch-top for hanging were made of pine and could be classed as country mirrors. Between

LEFT: Miniature looking glass with wood frame covered with gold embossed-and-figured paper. Flower spray painted on glass above mirror. Height 7¾ inches; width 4⅝ inches. American, 1800-1850. *(Courtesy Henry Francis du Pont Winterthur Museum)*

CENTER: Miniature looking glass; overhanging cornice, rope molding; gilded. Height 11½ inches; width 9⅟₁₆ inches. English or American, 1815-1840. *(Courtesy Henry Francis du Pont Winterthur Museum)*

Miniature cheval glass, mahogany; square, tapering posts with brass urn finials and trestle bases. American, 1800-1900. Height 8¾ inches; width 5¾ inches. *(Courtesy Henry Francis du Pont Winterthur Museum)*

1810 and 1820 a type of looking glass with an overhanging cornice upheld by columns and embellished with a painted top panel was made in both large and miniature sizes. The wood was painted and gilded.

A type of gilt looking glass with overhanging cornice with pendant balls and rope molding down the sides dates from 1815 to 1840. Large mirrors of this type usually had a painted top panel. Miniature looking glasses were also made of gold embossed and figured paper covering a wooden frame. These were probably made by an amateur and related to the wallpaper and painted paper frames on some early silhouettes. There were also miniature cheval glasses supported by turned posts and set on bases of various types. Over-mantel mirrors and very rare dressing-table glasses with several small drawers were also made in miniature.

Miniature Courting mirror.
Height 7 inches; width 5½ inches.

In America after the mid-nineteenth century miniature furniture was for the most part made by toy manufacturers and turned out in quantity. However, there was a group of artisan-craftsmen in South Hingham, Massachusetts, who organized themselves into the Tower Toy Guild. They were producing wooden toys including furniture in the 1850's but probably started work in the 1830's. William S.

Tower was the organizer and Cushing, Hersey and Augustus L. Hudson were other makers of miniature furniture associated with him. Daniel Litchfield carved miniature grandfather's clocks and Ralph T. Jones was making colonial doll furniture as late as 1915. Miniature furniture made by members of the Tower Toy Guild can be seen in Essex Institute in Salem and in the Old Ordinary in South Hingham. The pieces include cradles, desks, settles, ladder-back and Windsor chairs, poster beds and other bedroom furniture and drop leaf tables. Although made as toys they were hand crafted and are of good workmanship. Miniatures which are exact reproductions of colonial Windsor chairs, gateleg tables and poster beds are still being made so that the collector must be very careful. Many of these pieces are, however, of better workmanship than some of the older pieces.

Little is known about the makers of miniature furniture since few pieces are signed or labeled. From the workmanship of some pieces we know that they were made by a trained cabinetmaker, but no pieces can be definitely traced to any of the well-known cabinetmakers. Of course, there exists the story that miniatures were made by Chippendale in England and that Duncan Phyfe in America made miniature furniture. Of the known signed pieces the names are often second-rate local cabinetmakers or amateurs. However, a name and especially a date does add interest and value to a piece. Such an inscription might be written in a drawer or at the back of a cabinet or in the under framework of a chair. The earliest such paper signature was found on an American chest made by Archibald Grant in 1771. However, a rare miniature Chippendale chest of curly maple with the date 1764 carved in the top of the chest was recently advertised by a Pennsylvania dealer. It measures 20¼ high by 12¾ deep by 20 inches wide. The various toy furniture makers of the Tower Guild of Hingham, Massachusetts, used paper labels on their furniture. Labels of Samuel Hersey, Loring Cushing and Augustus L. Hudson have been found on miniature furniture made in Hingham, Massachusetts. Julius Lyon signed an American miniature chest of drawers in 1815 and a label of Charles B. F. Smith dated 1837 was found on a chest made in Delaware.

Silver

EARLY IN ITS EXISTENCE THE SILVER MINIATURE OR SILVER TOY AS IT was then called captured the interest of both the craftsman who made it and the customer for whom it was made. The miniature enjoys the same popularity with collectors today. Antique silver miniatures are inviting to the collector for, although the field is a limited one, there are enough examples to make collecting intriguing. While there is a profusion of later Dutch and Victorian pieces, both Dutch and English miniatures of the seventeenth and eighteenth century are rare. In spite of the controversy as to whether these miniatures were made as samples, apprentices' models or toys, such an authority as Sir Charles Oman believes that the most of them were made as toys—some few for the dolls' house, others for the use of dolls or child's playthings, but still others for the pleasure of an adult collector. His conclusions are based partly on size, the majority of them being too large for a dolls' house, also the most of them were too fragile to be played with. However, we do know that as early as 1571 Claude de France, Duchesse de Lorraine, daughter of Henry II of France, gave silver household miniatures to the child of the Duchess of Bavaria, and both Louis XIII and Louis XIV played with silver soldiers and little silver cannon. Although the royal children of France played with various kinds of miniature silver articles few of these are in existence today. These miniatures along with other silver were melted down in the seventeenth and eighteenth centuries when France needed funds to finance her wars. Many of these miniatures were undoubtedly made by French silversmiths but they were not generally available to children until the late eighteenth or early nineteenth century.

56

A few years ago a complete dinner service of miniature silver said to have been made for the King of Rome came on the market. It consisted of 200 pieces of silver and silver gilt including plates, pitchers, platters, serving dishes, a teapot, coffeepot, cups and saucers as well as a dozen knives, forks and spoons. The pieces had the French hallmark of 1819-1830.

In England there were silver miniatures in the dolls' house that Queen Anne gave to her godchild Ann Sharp and in several other English dolls' houses of the seventeenth century. The important books on silver usually neglect the silver miniature but there are enough silver miniatures in museums and shops today to convince one that miniatures were at one time made in considerable quantities.

DUTCH AND GERMAN

THE silver miniature was first made in Holland and Germany. The Netherlands is given the credit for initiating the silver miniature. The Leeuwarden silversmiths of Friesland were making miniatures in the fifteenth, sixteenth and seventeenth centuries. By the seventeenth century the silversmiths of Amsterdam, Haarlem, The Hague and other Dutch cities were also making miniatures. Dutch miniatures were plain, engraved and embossed. The earliest silver toys were martial—soldiers, cannon, arms. There were few silver utensils before the seventeenth century. Articles made at the end of the eighteenth century include kitchen utensils such as measures, sieves and cookie molds. There were also articles of hollow ware including coffeepots, teapots, hot water kettles on stands, pitchers, baskets, brandy warmers, cups and saucers, tiny boxes and many other pieces. The majority of the early pieces have plain surfaces with the only decoration being panelling, a fluted or beaded border at the termination of a foot or on the edge of a tray, and a bird's beak at the end of the spout on a coffeepot. The pieces that are engraved have simple scroll and floral designs. Early filigree work was characteristic of Leeuwarden. Dutch miniatures also include cabinets, chairs,

Group of miniature Dutch silver filigree toys. 18th Century. *(Taylor & Dull photo)*

cradles, sleighs, windmills, figures of a coach and horse, a sled and oxen, a lamp lighter, wells with buckets, tavern groups, ships and canal scenes. Many of these were of wire filigree or ornamented with cast all-over decorations. Some of this type of miniatures are antique but they are also being made for the tourist trade today.

Dutch silver usually has the mark of the city where it was made, the date and the mark of the individual silversmith. It is difficult to read the Dutch hallmarks. However, they can be easily distinguished from the English since they include such objects as the stork, deer, goat, fish, swan, rabbit, horn, hatchet, mermaid, crowned key, lion and key and acorn. The horn mark is one of the earliest (c. 1752), while the rabbit mark was used between 1798-1811. Amsterdam silversmiths whose marks have been found on

Dutch miniature hollow-ware. Amsterdam mark, late 18th Century. *(Ashmolean Museum, Oxford)*

Dutch miniature silver with Amsterdam marks. Rare ball tea urn and brazier. *(Ashmolean Museum, Oxford)*

eighteenth century Dutch miniatures include Willem van Straut 1741, Arnoldus van Geffe 1738, Roelof Helwig, H. Nieuwenhuyse, Reynier Brandt, D. W. Rethmeyer, and W. Warneke. Eighteenth century silversmiths of The Hague who made miniatures include Nicholaas Radijas, Cornelis de Haan, Reynier de Haan, G. van der Toorn, J. van de Toorn, Godert van Ysseldijk, F. M. Simons and

Toy silver spoon. Dutch, 1802. *(The Metropolitan Museum of Art)*

Miniature silver globular teapot with wooden handle and domed lid with wooden finial. Continental Europe, 1725-1790. *(Courtesy Henry Francis du Pont Winterthur Museum)*

Miniature creamer with globular body and tall curving neck. Height 1¹³⁄₁₆ inches. Continental Europe, 1725-1850. *(Courtesy Henry Francis du Pont Winterthur Museum)*

Miniature scissor-type sugar tongs. Length
3 inches. Europe, 1750-1850. *(Courtesy
Henry Francis du Pont Winterthur Museum)*

Miniature silver tea caddy. Height 1½
inches, width 1 inch. Probably English,
1720-1800. Maker's mark on base "DB".
*(Courtesy Henry Francis du Pont
Winterthur Museum)*

Jacques Tuiller. W. Dominicus of Leeuwarden made miniature
silver c. 1767. These names were found on pieces in the collection
of Lady Henriques in the Ashmolean Museum, Oxford, England;
in the collection of E. Schliemann, Hamburg, Germany, and the
collection at the Essex Institute, Salem, Massachusetts.

German silver miniatures followed the style of the Dutch
miniatures. They were first made for cabinet and dolls' house
display. A group of seventeenth century South German miniature
silver articles is in the Metropolitan Museum. These are made of
repoussé filigree. The tiny pieces consist of household furnishings
including a cabinet, a set of six peasant-type chairs, a bed, a
cradle, candlesticks, vases, a chandelier, a birdcage and a spinning wheel. There is also a carriage and a sleigh. There is little

Miniature silver candlesticks with hexagonal
stepped bases, turned shaft with knops.
Height 2⅜ inches. Germany, 1715-1740.
*(Courtesy Henry Francis du Pont
Winterthur Museum)*

Group of miniature South German silver, repoussé-filigree decoration, 1765-1800.
(The Metropolitan Museum of Art)

information about German silver miniatures. They may have been made in the Schwäbisch Gmünd district but more likely at Nüremberg or Augsburg since one of the first mentions of silver miniatures was of the toy silver soldiers made for Louis XIV in 1662 at Nüremberg.

ENGLISH

THE idea of making silver toys reached England from the Netherlands. However, there were no soldiers, coaches drawn by horses, windmills or sedan chairs which were so popular in Holland. Instead, English miniatures are usually utensils with a few exceptions such as the fireplace and articles of furniture.

During the reign of Charles II when silver was so widely used miniature silver became one of the extravagant novelties of the age and costly toys of gold and silver were the delight of sophisticates. This diminutive silver was made by silversmiths. The pieces of furniture, tableware and other household objects made in silver followed the decorative styles of the larger pieces in vogue. Silversmiths were meticulous in reproducing the detail and proportions as well as the style of the pieces. These small items are often paper-thin and it is amazing that they have survived. Some pieces show skill and finesse and are of exceptional workmanship. The early miniatures were often enriched with engraved ornament.

Often a miniature preserves a rare form, such as the chocolate pot with its stir-rod or "molionet," or the little silver plate stand. However, such a piece as the miniature still was a foible of its maker and probably not a copy of a larger silver article, and the miniature fireplace with its set of tools was also not a replica of a larger silver fireplace.

The early miniatures were enriched with engraved and chased ornament and some of the thin metal pieces were hand-worked from the plate. Units such as handles and feet were cast. Although some of the earliest pieces came from Holland, hallmarks prove that manufacture of English miniatures began as early as 1665. Completely hallmarked pieces belong to the late seventeenth century and the first part of the eighteenth century. While miniatures were never wholly exempted from hallmarking their small size often limited the marking and some pieces have only the lion passant gardant while other pieces bear only the maker's mark and some are not marked at all. Some pieces which were made as samples have only the maker's mark. Thus precaution should be taken when a

Group of English miniature silver. TOP SHELF: Teakettle and stand. Height 5½ inches. Edward Medlycott, 1748. Pair of sauceboats. Height 1¾ inches. John Le Sage, 1740. CENTER SHELF: Cruet stand, John Clifton. Bottles, Augustin Courtauld. Pair of sconces, Augustin Courtauld, c. 1720. Tankards, George Middleton, London, 1690. Candlesticks with reeded columns, square base. Height c. 2½ inches. BOTTOM SHELF: LEFT: Silver monteith bowl, London, 1708. Possetcup "M.A.," London 1700. CENTER: Spoon rack with spoons, George Middleton, 1684. Pair of tea caddies. Height c. 2 inches. England, mid-18th Century. FAR RIGHT: Basket, S. Herbert & Co., London, 1758. *(Courtesy The Philadelphia Museum of Art, Philadelphia)*

Comparison between some
of the miniatures shown
on the opposite page
and regular size pieces.

Group of English miniature silver. TOP LEFT: Brandy warmer. Height 1⅛ inches. Joseph Collier, Exeter, c. 1730. TOP CENTER: Teakettle and stand. Height 3⅜ inches. David Clayton, London, c. 1720. TOP RIGHT: Teapot. Height 1⅝ inches. London, c. 1720. BOTTOM: Plates, diameter, 2⅞ and 2⅛ inches. John Le Sage, London, 1720-1740. Teapot. Height 1⅝ inches. London, c. 1720. (*Courtesy The Henry Ford Museum, Dearborn, Michigan*)

miniature lacks the full series of hallmarks. The hallmarks are usually on the main body of the article. Naturally, the more complete the marks the greater the value. The hallmarked pieces are usually heavier and likely to be of better workmanship. While some silver miniatures are of the finest craftsmanship and possess elegance and style, there are many poorly made pieces, but this does not detract from their value because miniatures are treasured for their charm, rarity and interest and not for their technical perfection. The majority of English silver miniatures were made between 1684 and 1740 and

Group of English miniatures. TOP ROW: Saucepan with turned wooden handle. Height 1 inch. Joseph Collier, Exeter, c. 1730. Teakettle and stand. Height 3½ inches. Augustin Courtauld, London, c. 1720. Baluster candlestick. Height 2¾ inches. c. 1750. CENTER ROW: Mug with molded strap handle and moldings at base and rim. Height 1⅛ inches. John Clifton, c. 1713. Colander, diameter 1⁹⁄₁₆ inches. Gridiron, length 3¾ inches, 18th Century. Cup and saucer, John Clifton, c. 1713. Snuffers. Length 2⁵⁄₁₆ inches. Late 17th Century. BOTTOM ROW: Vinaigrette, Cocks & Bettridge, Birmingham, c. 1805. Length 1 inch. Pepper pot. Height 1¹⁄₁₆ inches. c. 1710. Long-handled frying pan. Length 4⅞ inches. John Le Sage, 1720-1740. Mid-rib teaspoon. Length 3⅛ inches. John Gibbons, 1725. *(Courtesy The Henry Ford Museum, Dearborn, Michigan)*

Miniature cup, circular bulbous form with scroll handles, gadrooned base, engraved scallops with border of engraved flowers. Height 1¾₁₆ inches. England, c. 1709-1710. *(Courtesy Henry Francis du Pont Winterthur Museum)*

Miniature silver salver, square with shaped edge, 3 inches square. England, c. 1724. *(Courtesy Henry Francis du Pont Winterthur Museum)*

nearly all of them were made in London. The making of silver miniatures seems to have been confined to silversmiths who made a speciality of the production of silver toys to the exclusion of larger pieces.

Silver miniatures were made by a great number of silversmiths; pieces with marks of over fifty makers of the early period between 1665 and 1739 have been found. However, there was a small group of men who specialized in miniatures and made the majority of the tiny pieces. The mark "GM" in various forms appears on the majority of the early pieces. This mark has been assigned to George Middleton, and the pieces made by Middleton date between 1684 and 1697. Middleton was the most important of the early miniature makers. He made miniatures of many types of articles, including furniture and fireplaces. A spoon rack holding six miniature spoons which dates 1684 is in the Philadelphia Museum of Art, but by far the largest collection of pieces by Middleton is in the Metropolitan Museum of Art. These include a silver whiskey still, a fireplace, grate, fire dogs, fender, shovel and tongs, a set of chairs and daybed in the Charles II style, candlesticks, silver snuffers, a posset pot and stand, a punch bowl and ladle, porringers, and silver tankards.

The unidentified silversmith "MA" also worked in the seventeenth century. His pieces are similar to those of Middleton and include the same range of articles, including coffee- and teapots, kettles, braziers and stands, tea caddies and flagons. A tiny two-handled silver cup with cover in the Philadelphia Museum of Art is hallmarked c. 1700, "MA," London. Another early maker was John Clifton, whose toys date from 1709. Clifton was also a prolific worker, producing many types of articles from fireplaces to complete tea sets. A unique piece by Clifton is the cruet stand.

In the second period of miniature making the field is dominated by two prolific workers: Augustin Courtauld and David Clay-

Miniature silver chocolate pot, lighthouse type, straight spout, wooden handle, domed cover with hole in top for stirring. Height 2¼ inches. England, c. 1725-1775. *(Courtesy Henry Francis du Pont Winterthur Museum)*

Miniature helmet-shaped creamer with engraved swags. Height 1¹⁵⁄₁₆ inches. c. 1784. *(Courtesy Henry Francis du Pont Winterthur Museum)*

Two miniature coffeepots, Queen Anne style. Height 2½ inches. David Clayton, London, 1709. The one on left, silver gilt. *(The Folger Coffee Company Collection)*

Queen Anne miniature coffeepot. Height 3½ inches. Robert Keble, London, c. 1710. *(The Folger Coffee Company Collection)*

ton. The many pieces of silver miniatures made and owned by the Courtauld Family are illustrated in a book *Silver Wrought by the Courtauld Family* by E. Alfred Jones. The illustrations include a miniature tea set with pear-shaped coffeepot, tea caddy, cups and saucers and rat-tail spoons. There is also a kettle and stand, a fireplace with tools and gridiron. These articles range from 2 inches to 3½ inches in height. The fireplace is 4¼ inches high and trays range

George I miniature coffeepot with molded and incised decoration Height 3½ inches. Joseph Daniel, London, 1719. *(The Folger Coffee Company Collection)*

George I miniature coffeepot. Height 3¼ inches. Augustin Courtauld, c. 1726. *(The Folger Coffee Company Collection)*

George I miniature coffeepot. Height, 2¼ inches. Augustin Courtauld, London, c. 1724. *(The Folger Coffee Company Collection)*

from 3⅛ inches to 5¼ inches square. Candlesticks with hexagonal baluster stem and circular foot are 2¾ and 3⅜ inches high. A beautiful little tea caddy 3½ inches high by Louisa Courtauld and George Cowles 1773 is in the Victoria & Albert Museum. However, although we know that the Courtauld family of silversmiths were makers of

George II miniature coffeepot with band of engraved trellis. Height 3⅛ inches. Paul de Lamerie, London, 1728. *(The Folger Coffee Company Collection)*

George II miniature coffeepot. Height 3¼ inches, c. 1740. *(The Folger Coffee Company Collection)*

miniatures, many miniatures marked with the Gothic letters "ac" have now been attributed by Sir Charles Oman to David Clayton as is also the mark "CL" originally given to John Clifton. Thus, according to Oman, David Clayton must have been by far the largest English manufacturer of silver toys. His work is all in Queen Anne style and dates from 1697 to about 1740. A 3 inch table with tripod legs, a warming pan with wooden handle and a trivet, all by David Clayton, are in the collection of Joseph M. and Aimée Loeb May at the Metropolitan Museum of Art. After Clayton stopped work the manufacture of silver miniatures declined sharply and was practically dead in England by 1750. It was revived at the end of the century and continued into the nineteenth century. The later pieces were usually spun and cast while early pieces were hand hewn.

Between 1690 and 1720 there were many miniatures made that bear only the unidentified maker's initials. Between 1725 and 1750 makers whose miniatures have been found include John Le Sage, Isaac Malyn, an apprentice of Augustin Courtauld, John Cafe and Edward Medlycott. A fine silver kettle and stand by John Le Sage, c. 1735, has a ball-shape plain body embellished with a band of flat chasing, plain scrolled legs and a straight gadroon edge. The kettle in the Philadelphia Museum of Art was made by Edward Medlycott, London, c. 1748. The pear-shaped body is covered with repoussé decoration. A coat of arms is engraved in the center cartouche. It has a curved bird's-head spout. The stand has a pierced floral apron and scrolled legs with shell feet. Also in the collection of the Philadelphia Museum of Art is a charming pierced cake basket made by S. Herbert & Co., London, 1758.

The silver miniatures of the early nineteenth century were confined almost entirely to tea tableware. They were of much smaller dimensions than the earlier miniatures and were covered with engraving and chased decorations. Since they were often too small to require hallmarking few are marked. These late Georgian pieces include the silver-gilt cast and chased tea service that was formerly in the collection of Her Majesty Queen Mary. It is dated c. 1822. Late pieces in the Ashmolean Museum, Oxford, include a jug with fluted sides marked "M.S." London, 1822; a teakettle and stand marked Gothic "DB" and lion passant gardant; a knife and fork by Atkin, Oxley & Co., Sheffield, 1832, and a toast rack by Rawlins & Sumner, London, 1833. A silver-gilt teapot with cast Oriental floral ornamentation was made by Joseph Willmore of Birmingham, c. 1830. Willmore was a maker of caddy spoons, which also were listed as toys, so that it seems very probable that other caddy spoon makers may have made miniature silver. Miniature tea- and coffee-pots were made by Paul Storr and many lesser known English silversmiths of this period. Although there were few English silver miniatures made in Victorian times, some were exhibited at the Great Exhibition in 1851, and a few pieces continued to be made and are still being manufactured. Copies of older pieces are also on the market so that the collector should be wary of pieces without marks. A knowledge of the shapes and styles of different periods will also warn the collector against an article with a date before such shapes were made. Copies of miniatures are made in Holland, Japan, Portugal and England to meet the present-day demand for tiny objects.

AMERICAN

In America there were no toymakers but some of the best known silversmiths of the late seventeenth, eighteenth and early nineteenth centuries made miniature versions of their full-sized pieces. Although these miniatures are scarce, a few have survived and many of these are marked. The most interesting group are the silver toys belonging to Bethia Shrimpton of Boston. They are now in the Yale University Art Gallery. They were made c. 1690 but are unmarked and the maker is not known. They include a tankard, a caudle cup, a pair of candlesticks with clustered pillars and a snuffer and tray. However, there are a few marked American pieces that date from the late seventeenth or early eighteenth century. An early flat-topped tankard 3¾ inches high by Peter Oliver of Boston (1682-1712) is in the Worcester Museum. The Boston Museum of Fine Arts owns two miniature caudle cups, one by John Coney (Boston 1656-1722) and a similar one with the stamp of Paul Rivoire (Paul Revere Sr., 1702-1754). Both cups have curving sides, a paneled leaf surbase with chased leaf forms on a pebbled ground. They measure 1¼ inches and 1⅓ inches in height. The Revere cup is marked "PR" in a rectangle. A third cup, the smallest of the three, measures 1 inch in height. It is of similar shape but is divided by incised lines into four panels of flowers. This caudle cup has been attributed to John Edwards (Boston 1671-1746). In the exhibition of the work of Elias Pelletreau held in the Brooklyn Museum in 1959 a small miniature mug (c. 1750-1810) 1⅝ inches high, was marked "EP." This mug and a miniature tankard 1½ inches high by John S. Hutton (New

Silver toys belonging to Bethia Shrimpton. TOP LEFT AND RIGHT: Candlesticks with reeded column, lobed drip pan and nozzle. Height 2¼ inches. TOP CENTER: Tankard. Height 2¾ inches. CENTER ROW LEFT: Caster with molded base and rim, domed pierced cover and turned finial. Height 2 inches. CENTER RIGHT: Caudle cup. Height ⅞ inch. LOWER ROW: Candle snuffers and violin-shaped tray on three legs. Length of snuffers, 2 inches. Tray 3⅛ inches. English and American makers, 17th Century. *(Yale University Art Gallery, Mabel Brady Garvan Collection)*

York c. 1720) are owned by Dr. and Mrs. Eben Breed. A tankard by Samuel Edwards is in the collection of the Boston Society for the Preservation of New England Antiquities. Miniature cans were made by Ebenezer Moulton (1768-1824).

There were also miniature American silver teapots and coffeepots. A globular teapot with straight spout and wooden handle (c. 1786) by Samuel Bartlett is in the Garvan collection of the Yale University Art Gallery. A miniature straight-sided oval teapot with tapered spout, pearwood handle and knob, bright-cut swags of flowers and husk ornament was in a Parke-Bernet sale of February 8, 1941. It was made by Robert Evans of Boston (c. 1790) and is stamped twice with the maker's mark, "RE", capitals, in a rectangle. It is 5 inches in length. A coffeepot and can by Caleb Shields (Baltimore c. 1770) were exhibited in London in 1960. An American miniature tea service consisting of teapot, covered urn and creamer with tiny pyriform bodies with tooled bands of scallop shells was made by Edward Lang, Salem, Massachusetts (1742–1820). It was in a Parke-Bernet sale of January 24, 1953. Another bright-cut tea set

LEFT: Miniature silver mug. Height 1⅝ inches. Mark, "E.P."—Elias Pelletreau, 1726-1810. RIGHT: Tankard. Height 1⁵⁄₁₆ inches. Mark, "I.H."—John Hutton, 1720-1729. *(Both collection of Dr. and Mrs. Eben Breed)*

by Shepherd & Boyd of Albany (1810–30) is in the collection of Philip Hammerslough. The pieces are of classical form with bands of engraving at the rims. It is marked Shepherd & Boyd in a serrated rectangle and engraved with the name Catherine Walsh. It measures, teapot: H. 3⁷⁄₁₆ inches; creamer: H. 2⅞ inches; sugar bowl: H. 3⁷⁄₁₆ inches.

One of the most attractive pieces of miniature silver is the tiny basket. There are many Dutch and English miniature baskets but the only American miniature basket that has come to light is that made by Zachariah Brigden, Boston (1734-1787). It is decorated with a pierced border and beading and the handle has bright-cut engraving. It is 2 inches high and is in the Minneapolis Institute of Arts.

At least two pair of miniature American silver andirons are known. They are 2⅝ inches high by 2¹⁵⁄₁₆ inches in length and have a molded baluster stem with lemon finial and cabriole legs ending in snake feet. They were made by Pieter De Riemer, New York, 1738-1814, and are marked "PDR" capitals in oval. Identical pairs are in the collections of Philip Hammerslough and Mr. & Mrs. James O. Keene.

Miniature spoons are the commonest silver miniature. All patterns used between the end of the seventeenth and the middle of the eighteenth century are to be found. Tiny English miniature spoons were made to hang on silver racks or to fit in shagreen cases, together with small knives and forks. American miniature spoons also exceed the number of pieces of plate. The earliest recorded American miniature spoon is the rat-tail spoon made by William Whittemore, Portsmouth, New Hampshire (1710-1770). There are feather-edge spoons made by Enos Reeves, Charleston, South Carolina (1753-1807), and by John David, Philadelphia (1736-1794). Six miniature spoons in the Museum of Fine Arts, Boston, are attributed to Richard Richardson, Philadelphia (1793-1796). Joseph Lownes, Philadelphia (1780-1816) also made miniature spoons with bright-cut decoration and shell backs. A set of six are in the collection of John D. Kernan. Six miniature spoons by Moore & Ferguson, Philadelphia (1801-1804), have an egg-shape bowl, downward turned rounded handle

Miniature drum-shaped teapot with fine-cut engraving, wooden handle and finial. Height 5 inches. Robert Evans, Boston 1768-1812. *(Taylor & Dull photo)*

Miniature silver basket with pierced rim and fine-cut engraving. Height 2 inches. Zachariah Brigden, Boston, 1734-1787. *(The Minneapolis Institute of Arts)*

Pair of silver andirons with cabriole legs and snake feet. Height 2⅝ inches. Pieter De Riemer, 1738-1814. *(Collection of Philip Hammerslough)*

and bright-cut engraving. They are marked "Eva" in script in a medallion on the handle and have the maker's mark, Moore & Ferguson, in capitals in a rectangle on the back of the handle. They are in the collection of Philip Hammerslough. Another set of six 3-inch

Miniature silver tea set with bright-out engraving. Teapot 3⁷⁄₁₆ inches; creamer 2⅞ inches; sugar 3⁷⁄₁₆ inches. Shepherd & Boyd, 1810-1830. *(Collection of Philip Hammerslough)*

Miniature silver tea set on tray. Black, Starr & Frost, Gorham, c. 1920. *(Museum of the City of New York)*

spoons attributed to John Walraven, Baltimore (1771-1814), are in the Baltimore Museum of Art. Spoons by Thomas McConnell, Wilmington, Delaware (1768-1825), are in the Historical Society of Delaware.

There are quite a number of miniature fiddle-handle spoons made between 1820 and 1840 by various makers. An unmarked spoon of this type is in Jefferson's home, Monticello. Others were made by various silversmiths including William Cowan, Richmond, Virginia (1779-1831). A set of six fiddle-handle spoons together with a pair of sugar tongs made by R & W Wilson, Philadelphia (1825-1846) are in the collection of Philip Hammerslough. Four fiddle-handle spoons by William Tenney, New York (1828-1849) are in the Museum of the City of New York. Six spoons with pointed oval bowls, U-shaped neck and slender shaft are engraved "Sarah" and have the maker's mark "WWH," William W. Hannah, Hudson, New York (c. 1840-1848). These are in the Winterthur Museum as are several other spoons of the same type and date. One is engraved "Sweetheart," and a tiny $1^{15}\!/_{16}$ inch spoon is engraved "Lilly." Fiddle pattern spoons marked "Annie" were made by E. Stebbins & Co., New York (1836-1841).

Six miniature silver spoons. Richard Richardson, 1793-1796. Silver tongs. Jeffrey Griffith, Chester, 1750. (*Museum of Fine Arts, Boston, Massachusetts*)

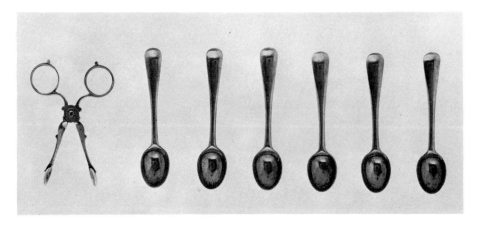

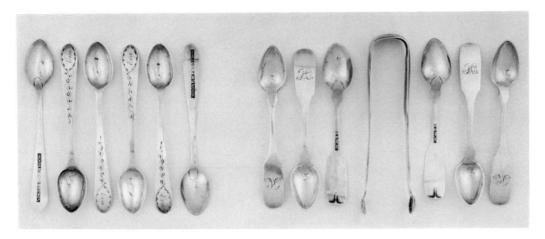

Miniature silver spoons. LEFT: six spoons with egg-shaped bowls, down-turned handles and bright-cut engraving. Moore & Ferguson, Philadelphia, 1801-1804. RIGHT: six fiddleback spoons and sugar tongs. R. & W. Wilson, Philadelphia, 1825. (*Collection of Philip Hammerslough*)

There are a few collectors who have been gathering silver miniatures over a period of some years, but for some reason miniatures have been ignored by museums and also by the writers of important silver books. Within the last thirty or so years, however, several important private collections have been presented to museums in America and England and this has made it possible for the general public to enjoy these miniatures and has also stimulated the interest of collectors. One of the finest collections of English silver miniatures consisting of forty-two pieces was given to the Philadelphia Museum of Art in 1934. A large collection of over one hundred pieces is in the Metropolitan Museum of Art. There is also an extensive collection in Henry Ford Museum and Winterthur Museum. A collection of Dutch and English toys is in the Essex Institute, Salem, Massachusetts. The collection in the Victoria & Albert Museum in London was also acquired as late as 1939. Also in England is the fine group of Dutch and English miniatures in the Ashmolean Museum, Oxford, England. Collections of Dutch miniatures are also to be seen in the Rijksmuseum in Amsterdam and the Gemeentemuseum in The Hague, Holland.

Tin, Pewter, Brass, Copper and Iron

THE TERMS COPPERSMITH, BRAZIER AND BRASS FOUNDER ARE CONFUSING since the men who made brass and copper articles were also often tinsmiths, pewterers or silversmiths and sometimes also even blacksmiths. The range of articles produced in the various mediums was wide. It included household articles such as pots and pans, fireplace equipment, lighting fixtures and tableware such as plates, cups, tea- and coffeepots and forks and spoons. All these items were made in miniature as well as regular size. They were made in the various countries of Europe and they were also made in America. Since few articles are marked it is difficult to assign the source or locality of any particular piece.

The miniature Nüremberg kitchens of the eighteenth century were furnished with pots and pans, ladles, spoons and skimmers of copper and brass, and graters, strainers and sieves of tin. There were also tin pudding molds, cookie cutters and candlesticks. The famous English pedlar dolls carried a full assortment of miniature tin utensils. In America in the early nineteenth century tin trays of various sizes and shapes were made with cut-work edges and Chippendale curves and were decorated with painted flowers or stencils. There were also tin kitchen utensils including teakettles, coffee- and teapots, scoops and graters. These were usually made by a local tinsmith. In the Pennsylvania Dutch country many of these small tin articles continued to be painted by hand. Tin cookie cutters were also made in miniature in various shapes including animals, birds and flowers.

Later tin miniatures were manufactured for gifts for tin wedding anniversaries. These articles included every type of utensil as well as tin hats, keys, spectacles and pipes. There were also many tiny tin cookie cutters made and these are available to collectors today.

Brass miniatures include fireplace tools, scuttles, teakettles, coffeepots, saucepans, spoons, cake, jelly and pudding molds. Brass candlesticks that screw into their bases were made in England in all styles from Queen Anne to Chippendale, Adam, Sheraton and Empire. These measure from 2 to 4 inches in height. Copper teakettles 3 inches high have brass finials and a removable top. Brass cooking utensils such as forks, skimmers and ladles have shaped iron handles.

There were also miniature iron pots, trammels, frying pans, waffle irons and small iron andirons. The majority of these miniatures date between 1800 and 1850. There were also miniature steel andirons with cabriole legs terminating in pad feet. The square tapered shaft was surmounted by a brass finial. Miniature tongs, pokers and shovels were also made, probably in England.

The toy Nüremberg kitchens seen in European museums show a complete array of such metal miniatures. There is also an American model kitchen in The Metropolitan Museum of Art which dates from the early nineteenth century and which includes miniature cooking utensils of metal and pottery which were made in America at that time. So many of these articles have been made for dolls' houses in recent years that the collector must beware of reproductions.

Miniature household articles of pewter were made in Europe as early as the seventeenth century. Complete tea and coffee sets including pots, plates of various sizes, covered dishes, mugs, steins, flagons and hot water kettles are among the pewter utensils made in Nüremberg from 1750 to 1850. Plates and platters had shaped borders and hollow wares were blocked or molded in swirl patterns. A miniature pewter tea set consisting of nineteen pieces includes a pear-shaped pitcher 1⅞ inches high, cups less than an inch high and saucers and plates with beaded rim. Miniature spoons with egg-shaped bowls measure 1¾ inches in length. The forms followed those of larger articles. Miniature pewter made in Nüremberg is usually marked. There are miniature pewter candlesticks with circular base and columnar shaft with Doric capitals measuring 2⅞ inches high, and another candlestick with saucer-shaped base, knopped shaft and bands of grooved decoration is 2 inches high. Both of these candlesticks are in the Winterthur Museum and date 1770-1820. A pewter snuffer with elaborate handles and a long oval tray measures 4½ inches overall. This type was made between 1800 and 1835. There were also pewter measures of ½ noggin size.

Miniature Nüremberg kitchen with pewter, brass, tin and copper cooking utensils. German, 18th Century. *(Courtesy Victoria & Albert Museum)*

Miniature pewter dishes with embossed conventional patterns and leaves and a small platter with an embossed pig were unearthed in Revolutionary camps in New York. (See New-York Historical Society Bulletin 1920-21 vol. 4.) Although pewter was being made in America at this time it is not known whether these dishes were made by an American craftsman or were imported. However, miniature pewter dishes were advertised by the pewterer Robert Boyle of New York in 1781, "doll dishes, plates and platters."

A Nüremberg kitchen, 1673, showing miniature pewter. *(Courtesy Victoria & Albert Museum)*

Miniature fireplace with andirons and other utensils. Miniature pewter candlestick and tin candle mold. American, 1731. *(Philadelphia Museum of Art)*

Miniature wrought iron brazier with perforated sides, scrolled feet and turned wood handle. Height 2⅞ inches. France, 18th Century. *(Courtesy Henry Francis du Pont Winterthur Museum)*

Toy pots and kettles. Late 18th or early 19th Century. *(Essex Institute)*

Miniature copper pans. Diameter c.
2 to 3 inches. American, 19th Century
(Courtesy of The Henry Ford Museum,
Dearborn, Michigan)

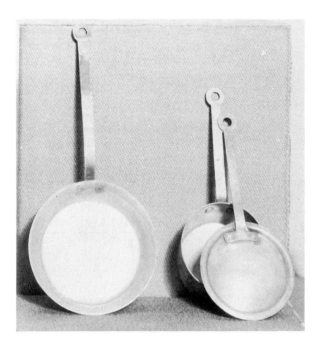

Miniature copper bucket. Height c.
2 inches. American, 19th Century.
(Courtesy of The Henry Ford Museum,
Dearborn, Michigan)

Miniature pewter teakettle. Height
1⅛ inches. England, 1725-1775. *(Courtesy*
Henry Francis du Pont Winterthur
Museum)

Miniature pewter beaker. Height 1⁹⁄₁₆ inches. American, 1750-1825. *(Courtesy Henry Francis du Pont Winterthur Museum)*

Miniature pewter tankard. American, c. 1840. *(Courtesy Henry Francis du Pont Winterthur Museum)*

Miniature pewter tea set with beaded borders. (9 pieces) Height 1⁷⁄₁₆ inches. Europe, 1860-1920. *(Courtesy Henry Francis du Pont Winterthur Museum)*

Miniature tin "lighthouse" coffeepot painted red. Height 2⅞ inches. Pennsylvania, 1830-1860. *(Courtesy Henry Francis du Pont Winterthur Museum)*

Miniature tin teapot painted blue with red, white, yellow and black floral decoration. Height 2⅜ inches. Pennsylvania, 1830-1860. *(Courtesy Henry Francis du Pont Winterthur Museum)*

Miniature covered tin pail with red, green and yellow painted floral decoration. Height 2 inches. Pennsylvania, 1830-1860. *(Courtesy Henry Francis du Pont Winterthur Museum)*

Miniature tin tray painted red with black edge and white flowers with black leaves and green stems. Length 4 inches. American, 1830-1860. *(Courtesy Henry Francis du Pont Wintherthur Museum)*

Miniature tin cup painted yellow, blue and red; daisy and leaves. Height 2 inches. American, 1830-1860. *(Courtesy Henry Francis du Pont Winterthur Museum)*

Miniature tin tray painted blue with yellow border and floral decoration in red, yellow and green. Length 4⁹⁄₁₆ inches. Pennsylvania, 1830-1860. *(Courtesy Henry Francis du Pont Winterthur Museum)*

In about 1800 James Dixon & Sons of England made pewter of a superfine grade and gave it the name Britannia. Britannia was made by the spinning process and this made a harder, lighter product. The tall coffeepot, the pigeon-breasted teapot and the whale

Miniature Britannia teapot. Height 3⅞ inches. *(Courtesy Henry Francis du Pont Winterthur Museum)*

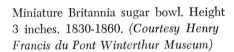

Miniature Britannia sugar bowl. Height 3 inches. 1830-1860. *(Courtesy Henry Francis du Pont Winterthur Museum)*

Miniature pewter snuffer and tray. Tray length 4⁷⁄₃₂ inches. Snuffer length 3¼ inches. Continental Europe, 1800-1835. *(Courtesy Henry Francis du Pont Winterthur Museum)*

oil lamp are typical Britannia pieces. These were all made in miniature. Britannia was made in America as early as 1810 but any miniature pieces were made some years later. There were miniature or "sparking" lamps of Britannia 4½ inches high with bell-shaped base

Pair of miniature Britannia lamps.
Height 1¾ inches. American, 1835-1865.
*(Courtesy Henry Francis du Pont
Winterthur Museum)*

Miniature Britannia lamp. Height 1⅜
inches. American, 1835-1865. *(Courtesy
Henry Francis du Pont Winterthur
Museum)*

Miniature Britannia lamp,
electrified. *(Courtesy Henry
Francis du Pont Winterthur)
Museum)*

Miniature Britannia lamp. Height 4½
inches. American, 1820-1860. *(Courtesy
Henry Francis du Pont Winterthur
Museum)*

LEFT: Miniature pewter candlestick, columnar shaft with Doric capital. Height 2¹⁵⁄₁₆ inches. European, 1770-1820. (*Courtesy Henry Francis du Pont Winterthur Museum*)

RIGHT: Pair of miniature pewter candlesticks with vase-shaped shaft and square base. Height 3⅞ inches. European, 1810-1830. (*Courtesy Henry Francis du Pont Winterthur Museum*)

and cylindrical font. As early as 1829 Boardman & Hart, well-known pewterers of New York, advertised children's plates, cups and nursing bottles, but miniature tea sets were made later in the century. There are several types of miniature Britannia tea sets. Some are plain except for a contrasting bright band, others have convex and concave bulges and may be decorated with beaded or gadroon borders. Roswell Gleason, the pewterer, is known to have made a tea set for his daughter, but pewter and Britannia tea sets of miniature size were not made in quantity until after the middle of the nineteenth century. In 1875 James W. Tufts, Boston manufacturer of silver plate, advertised children's Britannia tea sets in *Youth's Companion*. Similar

LEFT: Pair of miniature brass candlesticks. Circular domed base decorated with reeds and raised dots. Plain columnar stem with bands of same decoration as base. Height 3¼ inches. France, 1900-1950. (*Courtesy Henry Francis du Pont Winterthur Museum*)

RIGHT: Pair of miniature brass candlesticks with stepped base. Height 1¾ inches. (*Courtesy Melissa Halpert*)

tea sets are shown in portraits of American children painted by Joseph Stock and others between 1840 and 1870.

Many articles of various metals were made for nineteenth century dolls' houses, but these were manufactured in quantity and were usually of inferior quality. Also, many brass miniatures are being made and sold today. The old handcrafted metal miniatures are rare and hard to find.

Pottery and Porcelain

ENGLISH

THE COLLECTOR CAN FIND ENGLISH POTTERY AND PORCELAIN MINIA-tures of several sizes in all the known types of china from early red-wares, slip wares, stoneware, salt glaze, Whieldon and creamware to porcelain and late ironstone. There are various types of wares which were made in practically all of the English potteries in the eighteenth and nineteenth centuries. Stonewares imitating German stoneware were made in England in the seventeenth century. Tiny mugs and bell-shaped cups measuring 2¾ inches were made in red stoneware or Elers Ware with applied and stamped decoration of prunus blossoms and horizontal reeding. Brown stoneware with reeding and slip decoration was made in the Nottingham district. Tiny mugs and cradles date c. 1740. Salt-glaze stoneware was decorated with deep blue applied flowers and birds. Stoneware continued to be made in the Nottingham section down through the nineteenth century when it was popularized by Doulton. Miniature mugs, ginger beer bottles and steins are found in Doulton Ware.

There are miniature cream-color salt-glaze jelly molds in shapes such as stars, triangles and squares with molded designs in their bottoms. There are also miniature plates and platters with raised polychrome decoration of fruit and flowers as well as teapots and complete tea sets with raised shell patterns. Whieldon Ware miniature tea sets in brown and cream mottled ware were often set on a tiny tray.

95

TOP LEFT: Miniature salt-glaze plate. TOP RIGHT: Miniature Leeds plate with leaf border. BOTTOM ROW: Miniature cups and saucers. Height 1¾ inches. Spode. *(D. M. & P. Manheim)*

Miniature Leeds pottery was made in pierced openwork patterns and creamware painted with a red and black pattern of wheat. Other Leeds pieces had feather edges with hand-painted borders. Tiny mugs measured 1⅝ inches and a tea set with a colorful hand-painted floral pattern included a covered bowl and tea caddy. These pieces date from the late eighteenth century. Later Leeds wares were made with designs of transfer printing in oriental patterns including the Willow Pattern. Luster was also made at Leeds Pottery in the early nineteenth century. The Leeds Pottery was in existence from 1758 to 1840. With all the catalogues and documentary material available concerning Leeds Pottery there is no mention of minia-

Miniature tea set with painted free-hand decoration. Height, teakettle 3½ inches; coffeepot, 4 inches. Leeds, 1788. *(Courtesy Otto M. Wasserman)*

tures or toys. However, miniature tea sets have been found, some with the same patterns as the larger pieces, but the handles, spouts and knobs of teapots and other pieces are simpler in design than those of the larger pieces. A miniature tea set in King's Rose pattern was made c. 1830.

Leeds ware was also made at other potteries such as the important Castleford Pottery that put out its own catalogue in 1794. This catalogue contains many designs identical with those of Leeds Pottery. There was a business connection between Swinton and Don Potteries and Leeds and their pattern books also list various types of earthenware along the same lines as Leeds Pottery.

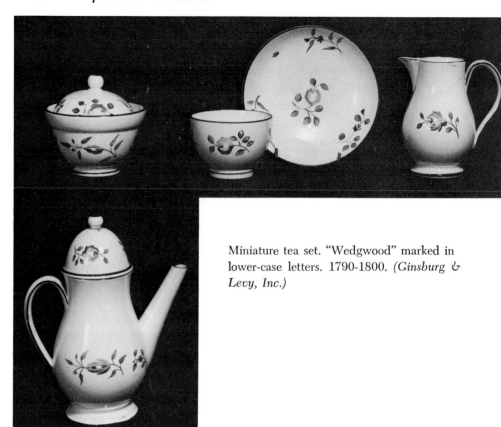

Miniature tea set. "Wedgwood" marked in lower-case letters. 1790-1800. *(Ginsburg & Levy, Inc.)*

Perforated creamware bowls and saucers. Height 1⅜ inches. Wedgwood, mid-18th Century. *(Collection of Dr. & Mrs. Stanley H. Greenwald)*

Wedgwood made all types of English wares, many in miniature, from early Whieldon types to transfer-printed wares. Cauliflower and other green glaze wares were made in small size sets in the eighteenth century and a few rare miniature 2½ inch cream jugs date from c. 1750. There was a miniature flower basket of cane ware with red relief of leaves made c. 1790. This basket is 4 inches long. A rare miniature buff-color cane ware tea set with fluted engine-turned design consists of a teapot, covered sugar and creamer, each piece measuring about 2 inches in height. Each piece is stamped "Wedgwood" in lower case letters. Creamware or Queen's ware was also first made in the mid-eighteenth century. In 1795 Queen Charlotte ordered "2 toy tea sets" of Wedgwood (Wedgwood London Ledger), and in the Wedgwood catalogue of 1817 creamware dishes are listed from 2 to 12 inches. Later in the century creamware and Jasper ware toys for children and small items for souvenirs are listed in the miniature field. Commemorative mugs and pitchers and copies of the Portland Vase were about 2 inches in height. There are minia-

Miniature cane ware tea set, buff color with vertical engine turning. Wedgwood, late 18th Century. *(Courtesy Otto M. Wasserman)*

Miniature cane ware tea set. Height of teapot c. 3 inches. Baskets with twisted handles and grape borders. Wedgwood, late 18th Century. *(Collection of Dr. & Mrs. Stanley H. Greenwald)*

ture tea sets, plates and tall tea- or coffeepots in delicate creamware with hand-painted borders. The plates are from 2 to 3 inches in diameter and the teapots about 4½ inches in height. The rare pink luster was introduced in 1805-1810 and there are extremely rare children's tea sets of this "Moonlight Luster." Porcelain was also first made by Wedgwood in the early nineteenth century. It was made with painted and printed patterns. However, the manufacture of porcelain was discontinued by Wedgwood in 1822 so that it is rare and probably not made in miniature.

Miniature Wedgwood children's sets have been found with a pattern of exotic birds printed in apple green with black edge. These sets have 2-inch cups and the dimensions of other articles are in proportion. Dinner sets in children's size were printed in one color and these miniature sets included the Willow Pattern printed in powder blue and a pattern of Asiatic pheasants.

The greatest number of Wedgwood miniatures are of Jasper and Queen's Ware. Jasper ware miniatures were first made with light powder blue and sea green grounds. Dark blue grounds are later. The colored ground is decorated with classic designs in white relief. Every type of classical shape is found in the Jasper ware vases from copies of the famed Portland Vase to covered urns with applied scroll handles. The subject matter of the white relief decoration is the same as that on larger vases and on bas-reliefs and medallions. It includes subjects from classical mythology including Apollo and Daphne; The Birth of Bacchus; The Birth and Dipping of Achilles; The Graces; Sacrifice to Hymen; Bacchanalian Boys; Aurora; Apollo and the Muses—all classic designs by Flaxman. There are also subjects by William Hackwood such as Cupids and Wreaths, Infants Playing, and The Dancing Hours by Hackwood after Flaxman. There are also the delightful designs of Domestic Employment by Lady Templeton and modelled by William Hackwood. These are scenes of mothers and children and there is one of a Shepherd Boy. The Infant Academy by Sir Joshua Reynolds was also a popular subject. Other miniature pieces have a decoration of acanthus leaves with scroll borders, grape and leaf borders, husk festoons and conventional

Pair of miniature Jasper ware vases, white relief scenes of Domestic Employment by Lady Templeton on pale green ground. Height 3 inches. Wedgwood, 18th Century. *(Collection of Dr. & Mrs. Stanley H. Greenwald)*

Black Basalt miniature teapot. Height 3 inches. Wedgwood, early 19th Century. *(Collection of Dr. & Mrs. Stanley H. Greenwald)*

anthemion designs. The vases range from 1½ to 4 inches. The remarkable feature of these Jasper miniatures is the quality of the workmanship. The detail and accuracy on even the smallest pieces is comparable to that on larger articles.

Miniature teapot, cream and covered sugar. Enamel flowers on back basalt ground. Wedgwood, mid-19th Century. *(Collection of Dr. & Mrs. Stanley H. Greenwald)*

Miniature blue and white Jasper ware cabinet pieces. Wedgwood, 19th Century. *(Collection of Dr. & Mrs. Stanley H. Greenwald)*

In addition to vases and ewers there were tea sets and small mugs in Jasper ware. These were made in dark blue throughout the nineteenth century and are still being made. Those after 1890 are marked "made in England." Wedgwood also made miniatures in cane ware, black basaltes and light red terra-cotta. The finest of these were made in the mid-eighteenth century. Cane ware miniature tea sets were decorated with linear patterns of geometric engine turning and also relief patterns such as Hackwood's infants. Black basalt or Egyptian ware was a fine black porcelain bisque and is finer than the basalt wares of other manufacturers. Many of the designs on basalt ware are of Egyptian inspiration. Basalt and terra-cotta bodies are also decorated with floral designs enamelled in the Chinese taste. These were made 1810 to 1850. Between 1858 and 1875 the ceramic painter Emile Lessore worked for Wedgwood. His delicate floral and

Miniature tea set on tray. Tortoiseshell Ware. Height, teapot 2¹³⁄₁₆ inches. 1745-1775. Staffordshire. *(Courtesy Henry Francis du Pont Winterthur Museum)*

Miniature stoneware tea set. Staffordshire, England, 1750-1770. Four circular handleless cups, 1¾₁₆ inches. Footed plate, ⅝ inches. Covered sugar bowl 2 inches high. Tall pear-shaped water pot, 2¾ inches. Globular teapot, 2⅜ inches. White bodies, enameled floral decorations in pink, yellow, green, red and blue. *(Courtesy Henry Francis du Pont Winterthur Museum)*

figure designs were painted on a deep cream body. There are miniature vases and candlesticks that were decorated by Lessore.

In the early nineteenth century miniature tea sets with painted decoration and pink transfers were made at Lowestoft. Tea sets with blue chinoiseries were also made at Lowestoft. Queen Victoria had a Lowestoft tea set with pink transfer scenes of mother and child. She also owned a miniature Leeds ware tea set. Liverpool also made child's tea sets in a pink transfer design of mother and child. Spode made a miniature set with a blue transfer Oriental design of a temple, trees, camel and man. The little plates were 1½ inches in diameter and the meat platter 6 inches. Another miniature Spode set had a design of yellow butterflies.

Miniature dishes with transfer-printed "Kite Flyers." Staffordshire, mid-19th Century. *(Courtesy of The Henry Ford Museum, Dearborn, Michigan)*

Many miniature tea and dinner sets of earthenware were made by the various Staffordshire potteries in the nineteenth century. A tea set decorated with blue cornflowers was made by Rogers c. 1800. There were also tea sets and miniature dinner sets in Willow Pattern. These had as many as fifty-five pieces, including plates of various sizes and covered bowls. Davenport made miniature tea and dinner sets in blue and brown transfer and in flowing blue and flowing brown. Miniature sets were also made in the various patterns of Spatterware, including Dove, Peafowl, Cottage, Dahlia, Rooster, Schoolhouse and Criss Cross. Little handleless cups are found in plain red, green, yellow or blue spatterware. There were also miniature sets in Gaudy Welsh, Ironstone with seaweed, and tea leaf patterns, as well as mocha ware and sprig patterns. These were late nineteenth century. There were tea and coffee services with blue transfer patterns illustrating the Pastimes of Childhood and in the mid-nineteenth century John Ridgway made a blue and white transfer Log Cabin Series. There were also black transfer scenes with children, dogs, and horses. These children's tea and dinner sets were made by the many nineteenth century English china manufacturers.

They are usually of the second size miniatures made for large dolls or the third size for children's use.

Between 1810 and 1825 a great number of small size miniatures were made in both earthenware and porcelain. The ewer and pitcher and the watering can were popular pieces. A miniature ewer in "Japan" pattern was made in Mason's Ironstone. William Ridgway and many other manufacturers made similar articles.

Miniature dinner set decorated with scenes of children's recreations. Plates, 4 inches diameter. Staffordshire creamware, early 19th Century. *(Courtesy Otto M. Wasserman)*

Spatterware, peafowl pattern, G. Adams & Son, mid-19th Century. *(Courtesy Otto M. Wasserman)*

Child's tea set. Tea leaf pattern. *(Mrs. Laura S. Ady)*

Miniature tea set with underglaze flower painting in blue. Height of teapot, 3⅛ inches. Staffordshire, marked "Rogers," impressed. c. 1830. *(Rupert Gentle)*

Miniature porcelain was made by the various well-known English companies, including Worcester, Caughley, Rockingham, Swansea, Bow, Chelsea, Derby, Coalport (Coalbrookdale), Spode and Minton. Caughley and Worcester porcelains with simple Oriental blue and white flower or landscape patterns were made in the eighteenth century. There were also tiny pieces in blue and gold, canary yellow and gold and painted "Japan" patterns. Teacups measure 1¾ inches. Later printed patterns included a milkmaid in brown and a black printed pattern of a girl and boy. Bow porcelain teacups in pink, green, blue and black measure 1½ inches and are decorated

Porcelain tea wares. Height, teapot 3 inches. Worcester, blue and white landscape scene. 1775-1800. *(Geoffrey A. Godden)*

Miniature tea wares, fisherman pattern. Height, teapot 2¾ inches; creamer 2 inches; plate 3 inches diameter. *(Geoffrey A. Godden)*

Miniature blue and white porcelain tea set. Height, teapot 3 inches. *(Arthur Ackerman)*

with a pattern of peonies and herons. There is also a purple print of a man and women with a cup 1⅝ inches, and a Chinese fisherman and a willow tree. These date from the mid-eighteenth century. Swansea miniature mugs are painted with birds and flowers. A tiny chamber candlestick has a garland of rose and yellow flowers and a mauve tulip. Most Swansea porcelains were made between 1813

Miniature cups and saucers. Height 1¾ inches. Spode, c. 1820. *(James K. Lewis)*

Three miniature porcelain bowls and pitchers with floral decoration and gold. Height 2 inches. Spode, c. 1820. *(Collection of Suzanne Stocking Mottahedeh)*

and 1817. They were decorated with fine flower painting in naturalistic colors and with "Japan" patterns.

Miniature Worcester baskets and vases were also decorated with flower panels on deep blue grounds and some hand-painted English scenes such as Worcester Cathedral and Malvern Abbey. These miniature baskets with painted scenes are marked Chamberlain Worcester and the title of the scene in red script. They date

Miniature porcelain pitchers. LEFT TO RIGHT: Green and gold. Height 2 inches; dark blue with light blue flowers; white with floral sprays; dark blue and gold with flower medallions; pink, white and gold with rose medallion. All Spode, c. 1830. *(Collection of Suzanne Stocking Mottahedeh)*

Group of miniature bowls and pitchers. TOP LEFT: Dark blue with gold and light bue flowers. Height 2¾ inches. Marked Spode and number in red. TOP RIGHT: Dark blue and gold with flowers on white. English, 19th Century. CENTER LEFT: Bowl and pitcher, "Japanese" design. Height 2 inches. BOTTOM: Bowl and pitcher, rose and gold. Height 1¼ inches. Rockingham, c. 1830. *(Collection of Suzanne Stocking Mottahedeh)*

LEFT: Miniature basket with gold decorations and center painting of Seat of The Earl of Bathhurst. Length 3 inches. Chamberlain, Worcester, 1813. RIGHT: Miniature basket with crabstock handle, centered rose decoration and raised gold acorn border. Length 2¾ inches. Spode, c. 1815. *(Collection of Suzanne Stocking Mottahedeh)*

Miniature baskets. LEFT: Basket with applied herbage and flowers on top edge, bouquets painted on sides. Height 1½ inches; diameter 3¼ inches. Marked Chamberlain Worcester. c. 1813. TOP CENTER: Potpourri basket with pierced cover, white ground painted with multicolor floral bouquets. Spode, c. 1830. BOTTOM CENTER: Oval two-handled basket, green with rose decoration. Height 1½ inches; length 3¼ inches. RIGHT: Basket with blue ground and floral bouquet in bottom. Height 1½ inches; length 3 inches. Spode, c. 1830. *(Collection of Melissa Halpern)*

c. 1813. Worcester also made vases with shell decorations and rare 4-inch vases on pedestals have painted feather decoration. There are also graceful ewers with deep blue grounds and panels of flower decoration and chamber candlesticks c. 2 inches in diameter.

Early in the nineteenth century porcelains decorated with colorful flowers and leaves in high relief were made at Coalport. These are generally termed Coalbrookdale. There are tiny covered bowls, teapots, creamers and sugar bowls encrusted with sprays of roses, carnations and blue convolvulus with rose finials. Floral encrusted baskets with handles and tiny shaped trays encrusted with flowers and birds were made c. 1820. Many of these tiny pieces are found marked "C.D.," "C. Dale"; "Coalport" or "Coalbrookdale" in underglaze blue. However, a large proportion of the later pieces were not marked. Coalport made more porcelain miniatures than any other company. These flower-encrusted porcelains were also made by Rockingham, Derby, Chelsea, Spode, and Minton in the 1830's. A rare miniature Derby papboat 2½ inches high has a rich blue ground and is encrusted with minute pink carnations and blue and yellow blossoms. Miniature vases were also flower-encrusted. There were also vases painted with flowers, English scenery and castles. A miniature Derby tea set with blue ground has white reserve panels painted with floral bouquets. The set consists of a teapot, covered

Miniature jug, green body, floral decoration. Height 1⅝ inches. Worcester, 1808-1820. Brown signature on base, "Chamberlains/Worc." *(Courtesy Henry Francis du Pont Winterthur Museum)*

Miniature teapots encrusted with roses, c. 2 inches. Coalbrookdale, c. 1820. FRONT ROW: Miniature creamer and watering can. Spode, c. 1830. *(James K. Lewis)*

Miniature teapot, lavender ground encrusted with flowers. Height 3 inches. Rockingham, c. 1830. *(Courtesy Otto M. Wasserman)*

Miniature watering can. Derby, c. 1820. *(Courtesy Otto M. Wasserman)*

Miniature cabaret set with floral decoration in color and gold. Spode, c. 1830. *(Courtesy Otto M. Wasserman)*

RIGHT: Miniature Rockingham teapot. 3 inches. *(Courtesy Otto M. Wasserman)*

BELOW: Group of miniature porcelain encrusted with flowers. Coalbrookdale, c. 1820. *(D. M. & P. Manheim)*

sugar, creamer, plates and cups and saucers. A similar Meissen miniature tea set with flowers on a white ground has the Marcolini mark. The manufacture of Derby porcelain began in the 1750's and continues to the present day. In 1890 the new company was appointed "Manufacturers of Porcelain to Her Majesty, Queen Victoria" and the porcelain became known as Royal Crown Derby.

Tiny Minton Rococo flower-encrusted ewers, urns, cottage vases and baskets with handles were also made at this time. These are of the Meissen type and are normally unmarked, but some pieces have a copy of the Dresden crossed swords mark in underglaze blue. Rockingham also made miniature flower-encrusted baskets in the 1830's. Some of these have center scenes of Sussex views—Brighton, Shoreham, Hastings and Worthing. Rockingham also made miniature porcelain spill vases with painted floral patterns. Similar spill vases were made by Derby, Spode and Coalport. Tiny chamber candlesticks measuring no more than 2 inches in width were also made in Swansea, Derby, Rockingham, Spode and other factories. A miniature Spode chamber candlestick with a diameter of 3¼ inches is decorated with a wreath of pink roses and delicate gold leaf scrolls. It dates c. 1790-1800. These tiny porcelain chamber sticks would make an interesting collection. They are rare but can be found in the various types of English porcelain.

Miniature candlesticks with green and pink flowers and gold bands. Height 1⅞ inches; base 1½ inches; rim ¾ inch. Spode, c. 1830. *(Collection of Melissa Halpern)*

Miniature urns; blue grounds, gadroon edges and floral bouquets. Height 2½ inches; width c. 2 inches. Marked Spode, c. 1830. *(Collection of Melissa Halpern)*

Pair of spill vases with gold leaves and bands and floral bouquets in pink, white and purple. Height 2½ inches; base 1¼ inches; rim 2¼ inches. *(Collection of Melissa Halpern)*

Miniature spill vases. LEFT: Chamberlain Worcester, lavender, with reserve panel of Malvern Abbey. Height 2½ inches; diameter 1½ inches. Marked, c. 1813. RIGHT: Vase with moss background and back panel with scene of Worcester Cathedral. Height 2¾ inches; diameter 2¼ inches. Marked Flight, Barr and Barr. c. 1807-1813. *(Collection of Melissa Halpern)*

RIGHT: Pair of spill vases, dark blue and gold with floral panel. Height 2 inches. Davenport stamped in red-brown and anchor. LEFT: Chamber stick, green and gold with pane of flowers. Diameter, 2¾ inches. Rockingham, c. 1830. *(Collection of Suzanne Stocking Mottahedeh)*

LEFT AND RIGHT: Pair of miniature porcelain spill vases with "Japanese" decoration. Height 2 inches. Derby, c. 1820. CENTER: Pair of miniature chamber stocks. Height 2 inches. Swansea, c. 1820. *(James K. Lewis)*

More miniatures are available in Spode than in any other English porcelain. There are miniature tea sets and cabaret sets decorated with gold and painted floral patterns against backgrounds of yellow, blue or rose. There are also tiny watering cans, baskets

TOP LEFT AND RIGHT: Pair of spill vases. Height 2⅛ inches. Coalport, c. 1830. CENTER: Spill vase, white with floral decoration. Swansea, 1810. BOTTOM LEFT: Miniature basket, Rockingham, c. 1810. CENTER: Miniature ewer, Swansea, c. 1810. RIGHT: Miniature bowl. Coalport, c. 1830. *(Courtesy Otto M. Wasserman)*

and spill vases and ewers and basins painted with fruit and flowers and bits of gold. Spode also made floral encrusted vases with roses, dahlias, convolvulus and cowslips. These were made c. 1820 and some are marked "Spode" with a number such as 2597. Cups and saucers are the most available pieces and these are in flower patterns and in colorful "Japan" patterns. The saucers measure 2 inches or

Miniature teapots. LEFT: Rockingham with green ground and a floral panel. Height, 1½ inches; width 3½ inches. CENTER: Worcester, blue ground and gold with multi-color flowers. c. 1820. RIGHT: Rockingham potpourri jar in the shape of a teapot with applied flowers. Height 1½ inches; width 3 inches. c. 1820. *(Collection of Melissa Halpern)*

Miniature bone china made for Queen Mary's Doll House. Each piece has Royal crest and monogram in burnished gold. Doulton, c. 1920. *(Doulton Inc.)*

Miniature clock; gold and white with black dial. Height 1⅞ inches; base 1½ inches. Marked Meissen. c. 1830. *(Collection of Melissa Halpern)*

Miniature tea service on tray. Gold decorations and floral encrustation. Tray 12 inches by 9 inches. Coalbrookdale, c. 1820. *(James Robinson, Inc.)*

less in diameter. Spode also made cream-colored earthenware printed in blue. Printed miniature sets were made by Spode and many other manufacturers in the nineteenth century including Stevenson, Ridgway and others. Ridgway also made toy floral decorated porcelain sets with coffeepots measuring 4½ inches high.

DUTCH

ORIENTAL blue and white porcelain of the K'ang Hsi period was popular in Holland in the seventeenth and eighteenth centuries and every Netherlander who could afford this expensive Chinese porcelain had a "china-room" filled with cabinets and wall brackets to display his collection. The cabinets, which recreated the Dutch

De Porseleinkamer in the Dutch dolls' house showing a collection of miniature Chinese and Japanese porcelain. 18th Century. *(Collection Haags Gemeentemuseum, The Hague)*

Miniature glass painted to represent Chinese porcelain of the K'ang Hsi and Yung Cheng Periods, early 18th Century. *(Collection Haags Gemeentemuseum, The Hague)*

Miniature Delft kitchen china painted with blue flowers. De keuken, Dutch dolls' house. *(Collection Haags Gemeentemuseum, The Hague)*

Miniature Japanese porcelain, 18th Century. *(Collection Haags Gemeentemuseum, The Hague)*

household in miniature, usually also had a china room which displayed a collection of Chinese porcelain miniature vases of various shapes as well as complete mantle garnitures and tea sets. There were also miniature vases and figures of "Blanc de Chine" with raised floral decoration. Japanese porcelain miniatures were also popular in Holland in the eighteenth century. Miniatures were also made in blue and white Delft. There are single vases and complete mantle garnitures in miniature sizes.

CHINESE EXPORT

CHINESE porcelains did not reach England in great quantities until the mid-eighteenth century when the English East India Trade was flourishing. The first American ship, the "Empress of China," did not sail for Canton until February 22, 1784. However, sets of Chinese Export Porcelain were probably used in America before this date. Although all sorts of Chinese porcelains were brought to Eng-

Chinese Export miniature mantel garniture; spill vases, 3¼ inches; covered jar, 4 inches. Famille Verte coloring, Chien Lung, c. 1775. *(Collection of Suzanne Stocking Mottahedeh)*

land, the Chinese Export Porcelain, that is, that with shapes and decoration influenced by English china, was the most popular and this is the type that is found in miniature sizes.

Miniature tea sets of Chinese Export Porcelain were probably first exported in the mid-eighteenth century. The shapes of the pieces are generally European and followed those of larger sets, as did the painted decoration. French porcelain with patterns of flowers and small floral sprays in the taste of English Lowestoft ware were copied on some sets. The teapot with round bowl, plain handle, straight spout and domed top was of Oriental inspiration and was the common form in the mid- and late eighteenth century. An early miniature set in Winterthur Museum has floral, fruit and leaf borders in rose

Miniature Chinese Export porcelain tea set with floral decoration and geometric borders. 1770-1785. (*Courtesy Otto M. Wasserman*)

Miniature Chinese Export porcelain tea set with coat-of-arms and spearhead borders. Type made for English market. 1770-1785. *(Courtesy Otto M. Wasserman)*

Pieces from Chinese Export porcelain tea set. Floral decoration, bud finials and twisted handles. Mid-eighteenth Century. *(Courtesy of The Henry Ford Museum, Dearborn, Michigan)*

Miniature Chinese Export porcelain tea set with floral sprays. Cups 2 inches. *(Courtesy Otto M. Wasserman)*

and sepia and another set has sprigs of gilt flowers and insects and butterflies in polychrome. The teapots are globular in shape with a circular foot, loop handle and straight spout. Tea sets with the cylinder-shaped teapot and interlaced handle were made about 1780. Many sets with tea pots of this shape had armorial decoration and spear-headed borders. Tea sets with painted landscapes and figures set within an oval usually had borders of Chinese emblems and date from the mid-eighteenth century. There were also miniature sets of Famille Rose design. These consisted of two teapots, a cream jug, teapoy, dish, spoon tray, bowls and eight or twelve cups and saucers. There were also other sets with as many as thirty-three pieces. One set made for General Knox of Revolutionary War fame had thirty-eight pieces. It had a cylinder-shaped teapot, helmet cream pitcher

and handleless cups. A sepia eagle emblem centered each piece and
the border was blue and gold. This type of tea set dates from 1790
to 1810. After the Revolution and during the Federal Era much of
the Chinese Export Porcelain for America was decorated with the
American Eagle, the insignia of the Society of the Cincinnati, scenes
of American ships, portraits and buildings such as Mount Vernon
or state capitols. A pair of late but rare miniature bowls in the
Winterthur Museum have a polychrome scene of the Declaration
of Independence with figures gathered around a table. The bowls
have a flower and vine border and sprigs of pink and lavender
flowers on the exterior on a white ground. The bowls are 2⅜ inches
in diameter and ⅞ inches in height. A leaf-shaped dish and a minia-

Miniature Chinese Export porcelain tea set with landscape and figures, c. 1750. Teapot, 2¾ inches; saucers 3¼ inches diameter. *(Courtesy Otto M. Wasserman)*

ture porcelain spoon have a similar scene and decoration. They are dated 1825-1850. Also in the Winterthur Museum is a miniature handleless cup and saucer (1780-1790) with a female head with bonnet and a border of gilt stars on a blue band. A miniature tea set with sprigs of roses on a white ground has both tea and coffee cups and a sugar bowl and cream pot with twisted handles and flower finials. It was made between 1775 and 1785.

Another Chinese Export Porcelain miniature tea set has a white ground decorated in deep blue and a landscape with small buildings, the sun and a flock of birds. The set consists of a globular form teapot with domed cover ending in a mushroom finial. There are miniature cups without handles and a slop bowl. The teapot is 3⅛ inches high and the cups are 1⅞ inches in height. The set was made between 1790 and 1800. Another tea set with teapot of cylinder form, straight sides and a straight spout and floral knob has a simple banded decoration in overglaze colors and gilt and a wavy edged border of blue with gilt stars. This set and one with a grape and vine border in gilt and sepia date between 1800 and 1815.

The many miniature Export Porcelain tea sets in the Winterthur Museum and in the recent advertisements of American antique dealers give evidence of the quantity of such sets that were made. Some of these miniature sets were probably stock items. In 1810 there were sets with transfer scenes of Bartolozzi's "Playing at Marbles." These sets were undoubtedly stock sets made for the English market. However, the existence of such sets with crests or monograms show that they could be decorated to special order. Also, a set with such a design as painted hearts flaming upon an altar of black and gold would surely have been decorated to order. That miniature tea sets were in demand is evidenced by the letters of instructions to the captains of ships and in the account books of the various merchants in the China trade. In 1788 Samuel Fleming wrote to Captain Randall of the ship "Jay" in Canton: ". . . purchase for me at Canton a compleat set of table china with the desert: white ground and violet colored border, as p the small specimen of silk, affixed with ware to border. . . . Purchase also a child's set for my daughter." In 1815 Catherine Elizabeth Peabody instructed Benjamin Shreve to buy and bring home in the ship "New Hazard" "a handsome set of (tea) China rather diminutive white with gilt figures. In a neat little Box to contain it when not in use." This may not have been a miniature set but in another memorandum in Shreve's notebook he records a doll's set as cargo for the ship "Governor Endicott": "D. L. Pickman wishes me to get a small dining set of ware for his children to cost 3 or 4 Dolls small number of pieces—if it cannot be had for that then buy a few pieces small ware—they have a tea set."

Miniature bowl and jug. Height 2½ inches. Vieux Paris, c. 1810. *(James Robinson, Inc.)*

Miniature French china sugar bowl and cups. *(D. M. & P. Manheim)*

AMERICAN

MINIATURE jugs, pitchers, crocks, mugs and bowls were made of stoneware, slipware and brown Rockingham in the various potteries of New England, Pennsylvania and Ohio. Whether these were made for children as some certainly were or to outfit a toy kitchen such as the one in the Metropolitan Museum of Art or whether they were made as souvenirs of a visit to the pottery is not known. Perhaps the answer is to be found in all three categories. Few of the pieces are marked and since there is a great deal of similarity between such products it is not always possible to assign a tiny piece to a definite section of the country. We do know that in about 1820 John C. Crolius made baby stoneware pitchers from ½ inch to 1½ inches in height. Other pieces of miniature stoneware date as early as 1800 and some continued to be made into the twentieth century. The majority of the pieces range from 1½ inches in height to 3⅛ inches high. The stoneware has a gray, blue-gray or beige ground, a salt glaze, and sometimes a floral or leaf free-hand decoration in cobalt blue. Some pieces have raised bands at base and neck. Pitchers have compressed loop handles and crocks often have lug handles. A few miniature crocks have been found with impressed names such as the 3-inch crock at Bennington Museum marked "Julia Ann Pratt." There is also a 3½-inch crock marked "J & E Norton." This was made between 1850 and 1859.

American red earthenware was made in small rural potteries. This reddish brown ware was decorated with glazes of earth colors such as brown, yellow, green and black. That made by German settlers in Pennsylvania and North Carolina was based on Old World peasant tradition. The tulip or bird motif was a typical design. Miniature pieces made included jugs and small plates, some with inscriptions. There were also redware pitchers 2¾ inches high with dark red-brown glaze and small demi-johns with manganese glaze. Others are of greenish yellow earthenware with tan spots or red splashed

Miniature red earthenware, second quarter of 19th Century. Pitcher greenish yellow with tan spots, New England. Bottle and handled cup, deep red splashed in brown, New England or Pennsylvania. Bowl splashed in brown and impressed "L. Kopp, Penna." Marked "ELMER" on one side and "1866/CROSS" on other. *(Courtesy of The Henry Ford Museum, Dearborn, Michigan)*

with brown. Redware was both slip-decorated and scratched or carved with a design.

Shenandoah Pottery was made by the Bells in Strasburg, Virginia, between 1833 and 1899. The pottery is streaked or mottled in gaudy orange red, olive green and manganese. The many forms included rare miniature pots and tea sets. The various Shenandoah potteries also made miniature cups and saucers and jugs with brown glaze. Stoneware flower pots measure 1¾ inches in height and a jug with green glaze is 1½ inches high. Tiny miniature platters 3½ inches in diameter are decorated with yellow slip and some bear inscriptions

Miniature stoneware crocks, United States, 1850-1940. LEFT: Low circular form with wide neck, rolled rim and loop handles, 1⅛ inches by 1⁹⁄₁₆ inches. CENTER LEFT: Low form with bulging sides, wide neck, rolled rim, loop handles and two narrow bands near base. Light gray, zigzag decoration in cobalt blue. 1¹³⁄₁₆ inches by 2⅞ inches. CENTER RIGHT: Tall cylinder form with rolled rim, loop handles; light gray with cobalt blue decoration. 1⁷⁄₁₆ inches by 1⅜ inches. RIGHT: Tall cylindrical form with wide neck, inverted rim and loop handles; light gray with cobalt blue decoration. 2½ inches by 2⁷⁄₁₆ inches. *(Courtesy Henry Francis du Pont Winterthur Museum)*

Miniature stoneware pitchers, United States, 1800-1940. Gray to gray-blue bodies with cobalt blue decorations. 2⅞ inches to 3⁷⁄₁₆ inches in height. *(Courtesy Henry Francis du Pont Winterthur Museum)*

such as "Sarah's Dish" or "Apple Pie." Many of these miniature dishes were made in Pennsylvania Dutch country but they were also made in New England and Mid-Western potteries.

An unique brown slip set of child's toy dishes consisting of a sugar bowl 1⅞ inches high, a cup 1⅛ inches high and a pitcher 2 inches high, now in the Bennington Museum, was made by John Harrison for the daughter of his landlady. There are also rare slipware miniature coffeepots and platters 3½ inches by 2½ inches with wavy yellow slip decoration.

Many miniature articles of various wares were made at Bennington from the 1820's through the 1890's. Richard Carter Barret in *Bennington Pottery and Porcelain* lists them under Novelty Items. They include pitchers, jugs and vases in the various wares, from stoneware and Rockingham to Parian. Although some of these must

LEFT: Stoneware jar, United States, 1800-1850. Circular elongated body, dull gray with cobalt blue leaflike decoration. 2⅝ inches by 2⅝ inches diameter. RIGHT: Stoneware crock, 1800-1900. Bulbous body with lug handles; gray salt-glaze body with blue floral decoration. 3¼₆ inches by 3¼₆ inches. *(Courtesy Henry Francis du Pont Winterthur Museum)*

Miniature Rockingham and Flint Enamel. TOP ROW: Rockingham cuspidor 1½ inches high. Tiny jugs ½ inch to 1⅞ inches high. Brown slip-covered cup and saucer. Cup 1¼ inches high, 2 inches diameter. Saucer 3½ inches diameter. BOTTOM ROW: Left, Flint enamel goblet 2½ inches high; Rockingham footed bowl 2¼ inches high; bowl and pitcher 3⅛ inches high; Rockingham jardinière 2¼ inches high. (*The Bennington Museum*)

RIGHT: Miniature pottery asparagus and cabbage. c. 2 inches. Thuringia. (*Merryvale, Inc.*)

have been sold commercially they do not seem to be listed in any catalogues or price lists. Miniature Rockingham and Flint Enamel items included tiny jugs from ½ inch to 1⅞ inches high, a flint enamel goblet 2½ inches high and a tiny pitcher and bowl. There were tea sets of common white pottery and Parian Ware but these are very rare and the only examples are in the Bennington Museum.

Miniature Parian porcelain pitchers ranged in size from 1 inch to 4 inches high. They were made with the various ornamentation used on larger vases, including corn, grapes, shell and floral motifs as well as profiles, figures and animals in relief such as a dog and a rabbit. These were made in both white, and blue and white.

Rare Parian miniature baskets with applied flowers made by John Harrison, 1843-1845. *(The Bennington Museum)*

Miniature blue and white porcelain vases, 2¼ to 4 inches high. 1850-1858. *(The Bennington Museum)*

Miniature Parian porcelain pitchers with molded decoration, 1⅝ to 2¾ inches high. BOTTOM CENTER: Pitcher with applied grape decoration, 4 inches high. *(The Bennington Museum)*

Tiny hand-shaped vases were made as small as 2 inches high and miniature blue and white Parian "cottage" vases with molded grapes were 2½ inches high. There were also tiny 3-inch Rockingham chests of drawers and a Rockingham cake mold 1½ inches high and 3¾ inches in diameter. However, the rarest and most fascinating of the miniatures made at Bennington were the Parian miniature baskets with applied flowers. These were not production items but were made for special orders. The baskets ranged from 1 inch to 2 inches high. They were filled with hand-made and applied flowers such as morning glories and forget-me-nots. Some baskets had handles and the basket itself usually imitated wickerwork. Most baskets were white but others had a few scattered blue flowers.

Glass

ENGLISH AND CONTINENTAL

GLASS MINIATURES WERE FOUND AMONG THE EXCAVATIONS IN EGYPT and Greece. These were some of the pieces which fascinated Louis Tiffany and led him to imitate them in his Favrile glass. In the Middle Ages miniature glass was made in Italy, Germany and Holland. The Germans began making glass in the fourteenth century. They imitated Venetian models but the glass was coarse and heavy in comparison although workmen were imported from Murano. The Dutch also made glass in the Venetian style.

In the eighteenth and nineteenth century glass toys were made in Bavaria and Bohemia, especially in Passau. This glass was hand blown in the Italian tradition with applied bands, fancy finials and handles, prunts and rigaree decoration. In fact, Italian miniatures of this type are more plentiful than those of any other country but they are also being blown today and are popular souvenirs of visitors to Murano.

All sorts of miniature glass toys were also made in England in the eighteenth century. In 1760 John Bench of Warwick made glass toys and C. Heady included "Toys for young Ladies" in his glass list of 1772. In 1785 Muson King of Manchester advertised "all sorts of glass toys in miniature." The making of glass toys was general at first but by the end of the century it was centered in Birmingham. In the Birmingham Directory of 1816 there were ten glass-toy manufacturers and by 1855 there were thirty-two. Thomas Osler, the well-known maker of cut glass, also advertised "glass toys and

pendants" in 1811. Much glass known as Bristol and Nailsea was made at Birmingham and the Nailsea Glass Works actually had a branch at Birmingham in 1824. This type of glass, Cesmibülbül, was also made in Turkey at the Beykoz Factory on the Bosphoros in the mid and late nineteenth century.

Group of hand-blown miniature glass. LEFT: Decanters, vases and candlesticks. RIGHT: Group of tablewares, Bristol type, opaque white with painted floral decoration. English and German, late 19th Century.

Group of hand-blown miniature glass. Continental Europe, late 19th Century.

In the nineteenth century popular taste had turned from clear to colored glass and there was a wealth of jugs, bowls and bottles in blue, green, amethyst and purple glass and striped glass. Many of the articles were made for sale at fairs and were for amusement and decoration. Such were the hats, boots, miniature pitchers and tea

Miniature glass tablewares
Nailsea and Bristol types.
Height, tallest piece,
c. 2 inches. Late 19th
Century.

Group of blown, cut and enamel decorated glass miniatures. Tallest bottle, 2⅝ inches. England, mid-19th Century. *(The Corning Museum of Glass)*

sets. Many of these articles were made in Stourbridge and North and Midland glass houses as well as those around Bristol. Miniature tea sets of Bristol-type glass included hand-blown opaque white glass hand-painted with pink roses and blue and gold touches and also royal blue, green and clear glass. These little tea sets were made in great quantities in Birmingham in the 1870's and 1880's. Nailsea type glass with latticino threads, loops, and strings was made in tea sets, small vases, pitchers and candlesticks. These tiny articles were also made with clear and opaque spirals of blue or pink. Miniature candlesticks were of both baluster and chamber type and the bases often had applied handles and other decoration. Wine glasses in Bristol blue measure from ¾ inch to 2 inches high. Decanters and water jugs were 1¾ inches to 3 inches high. Bristol and Nailsea glass miniatures are also decorated with painted red or green dots.

Small milk glass tea sets were also made in England in the early nineteenth century although milk glass jugs and quantities of striped miniature red and blue pitchers, vases, glasses and candlesticks were also made at Passau and in France at St. Louis and other French glass houses at this date. The manufacturers of England and the United States were close in style and technique in the mid-nineteenth century. There were also emigrant Stourbridge workmen working in such glass factories as Sandwich Glass Company and New England Glass Company.

There is a considerable amount of miniature glass on the market today and it is easy to find a small cup and saucer or vase but complete sets are rare and seldom available. Also there are many present-day hand-blown pieces made in Italy that are offered as antiques.

FRENCH

BY 1878 when Gallé exhibited his glass in the Paris Universelle Exposition, Art Nouveau was emerging as an influence in art, architecture and decoration. The furniture and backgrounds of the period provided space for collections, and mantels, cabinets and cupboards gave shelf space for ceramics, glass and other Art Nouveau accessories. Gallé was the most original and imaginative of the glass makers. His glass included crystal decorated with enamels and engraving in arabesque. He also made opaque colored and marbled glass as well as triple-cased glass with gold leaf between the layers of casing. Many themes were borrowed from antique glass and Arabian, Persian and Bohemian influences are seen. However, as time went on, it was the influence of his own native soil that dominated his design and on his vases we see the landscape, the trees, the flora and fauna of Lorraine. Delicate representations of water lilies, fern fronds, marsh-trefoils, forget-me-nots, dandelions, poppies and other wild flowers are represented in their naturalistic beauty. The use of flowers and insects shows the influence of Oriental art but Gallé's use of nature grew out of his own botanical interests. He said, "Yes, the different materials, forms, colorings and natural decorations all spring from contemplating the reality of nature. In my case new ways of handling and treating the glass have always arisen from new expressive needs. These innovations, which come into play after engraving, acid and glazes have had their turn are: glass inlay work, overlays of clear glass and intaglio glass." Gallé used various layers of cased glass to form his flowers and other decorative forms. The design was cut in relief with hydrofluoric acid and the finishing touches were put on by engraving. The acid left a satin finish but some pieces were polished to a smooth oily surface.

Gallé also experimented with colors. Much of the early glass was a smoky amber. Blue was produced by means of cobalt oxides. Finally, all colors were made, from orange and reds to violet and purples. White glass was mixed with a metallic base and pulverized glass of various colors in order to vary the shades of coloring and to obtain the transparent qualities of precious stones. Some vases have the opalescent greens of chrysoberyl or chrysolite, some the silvery gleam of cymophane, others the scarlet of cinnamonstone. Turquoise,

Gallé cabinet miniature. Golden orange leaf floral design on a camphor background. Height 4 inches; width 3 inches. *(Courtesy Sharp's 1860 Antiques)*

amethyst, sunstones, moonstones, opals, agates, sardonyx, garnets and various quartz and granite colors are seen in the imaginative glass of other vases.

There are several types of Gallé glass, those of clear glass with enamel are the earliest. The cameo or cased glass vases with flowers and leaves were the most popular type and probably made in the largest quantity. They were made in many different shapes, designs, and colors, and no two pieces were exactly alike. The earlier ones were richest in color and finest in design because they were created by Gallé himself or under his close supervision. Later vases were made in great quantities with a simple relief of one color on an opaque white ground. They were both polished and satin finished. Gallé vases range in size from large exhibition pieces as tall as 25 inches to small 2-inch cabinet pieces. While Gallé did not specialize in miniatures there are enough of the small pieces to interest the collector of miniatures. Such a vase as the transparent 2½-inch cameo vase with red and orange stems and berries would enhance any cabinet collection. Vases of similar design with carnelian berries and leaves on frosted yellow and carnelian grounds are 3⅝ inches and one with carnelian berries and leaves on a frosted ground with orange is 3½ inches high. A tiny perfume bottle has a cameo design of amethyst iris on a frosted white ground. There are also small 2½ inch covered boxes with designs of a dragonfly, pond lilies and reeds in amethyst on frosted amber. A similar design decorates a 3-inch vase. There are also tiny 3-inch cordial glasses signed "E. Gallé Nancy" that would fit in with a collection of miniature Art Glass.

All Gallé glass is marked and there are many different marks, each having a special significance. The marks are etched, cut and molded. Sometimes the mark is worked in as a part of the design. "Cristallerie de Gallé" etched, was an early mark, "Emile Gallé" and "E. Gallé" were later. Pieces made by the factory were marked "Gallé molded". After Gallé's death in 1904 the factory continued production of cameo glass until 1913, but the mark was "Gallé" preceded by a star.

P. J. Brocard was a contemporary of Gallé and his glass shows Gallé influence.

Antonin and Auguste Daum of Nancy were also influenced by Gallé. They reflected Gallé's use of Arabian and Egyptian designs and his later natural forms. Their vases have naturalistic asymmetrical designs of broad leaves stretched and elongated on slender-necked vases. However, the shapes and ornament are less imaginative and more sober than those of Gallé. They are usually simple ovals, squares and rectangles with an abrupt cut-off top without any lip. In texture the glass looks as if it had been hewn from a block and allowed to retain its roughness.

Although Daum made cameo glass vases with naturalistic floral designs he also made sepia windmill scenes on a cream ground. The most characteristic type of decoration was the winter or summer landscape scene with dark enameled trees silhouetted against a

LEFT: Miniature Cameo creamer shading from green to amethyst, ivy design. Signed, "Daum Nancy." Height 4 inches. CENTER: Miniature Webb Cameo vase, pink and white floral and butterfly design on lemon yellow ground, white lining. Height 2 inches. RIGHT: Cameo flower form, orange and yellow vase decorated flowers and ferns. Height 5 inches. Signed "Daum Nancy." (*Maude B. Feld*)

Miniature vase, signed "Daum, Nancy."
Height c. 4 inches. c. 1925. (*The Corning Museum of Glass*)

sunset sky of orange and yellow and a foreground of snow. The design has deep cutting on the trees and snow. Vases with spring landscape scenes have a mottled pale blue background. Miniature vases, of which many were made, range in size from 1⅛ inches high to 3 inches in height. There are also small bowls and vases 4 and 5 inches in height which might be included in a miniature collection. Vases are square, rectangular, and some have long narrow necks. Vases are signed "Daum, Nancy," with a cross of Lorraine. Other French Cameo miniatures were marked "Le Grass"; De Vez"; La Verre Française," and "Muller Frères, Lunéville."

Miniatures were also made at St. Louis. These were a striped candy cane type. Pitchers of various shapes were made in stripings of blue and white, pink and white, and green and white. There are also miniature ewers and bowls ranging from 2 to 4 inches in height and miniature footed compotes. These were made in the 1840's when the paperweights were made and there are tiny paperweight bottles with stoppers and rare miniature paperweights. Other European glass miniatures included decanters with stoppers and neck rings in clear and blue glass. In height they ranged from 1½ inches to 2¹¹⁄₁₆ inches. Amber glasses with handles and a white band at the rim were 1⅛ inches in height and a green pitcher measures 2 inches in height. Milk glass jugs striped in red and blue were made at Passau in the Bohemian Forest at this time.

LEFT: Miniature pink and white latticino creamer, St. Louis. Height 2¼ inches. RIGHT: Miniature latticino rose bowl with white "val" lace and pink ribbons. Nicholas Lutz. Height 2⅛ inches. *(Maude B. Feld)*

LEFT TO RIGHT: Miniature striped vase, blue and white. Height 2½ inches. St. Louis, mid-19th Century. Vase, white stripes with red rim. Height 2½ inches. Blue and white striped vase and saucer. Height 2¼ inches. St. Louis. Green and white striped vase. Height 2¾ inches. Dark blue striped pitcher. Height 2¼ inches. St. Louis. *(Louis Lyons)*

Miniature wine glass. Blown clear glass, circular bowl, double knop stem, flat circular foot. New York, 1775-1825. Height 2¼ inches. *(Courtesy Henry Francis du Pont Winterthur Museum)*

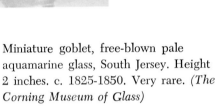

Miniature goblet, free-blown pale aquamarine glass, South Jersey. Height 2 inches. c. 1825-1850. Very rare. *(The Corning Museum of Glass)*

AMERICAN

FREE-BLOWN glass miniatures were made in the various American glass works in New York, New Jersey, Pennsylvania, New Hampshire, Vermont and the Mid-Western glass factories in Ohio in the early nineteenth century. There are tiny glass pitchers, mugs, bowls, decanters and wine glasses. They range in color from clear glass, blue and aquamarine to rare canary. A tiny pale aquamarine wine glass 2 inches in height has a double knob stem and a flaring applied circular foot. It was made in South Jersey. Another miniature bluish aquamarine wine glass 2⅝ inches in height was made in New York State. An aquamarine candlestick 3⅜ inches high was made at Lockport Glass Works, New York. There were miniature mugs measuring 1¹¹⁄₁₆ inches in height, 2⅞ inches rummers and 2¾ inches high mea-

Miniature mug; aquamarine, circular body, applied loop handle. Height 2¼ inches. American, 1800-1900. *(Courtesy Henry Francis du Pont Winterthur Museum)*

Miniature mug; blown three-mold pattern with band of vertical ribs and diamond diapering. Clear glass. Height 1¾ inches. Boston and Sandwich Glass Company, 1825-1850. *(Courtesy Henry Francis du Pont Winterthur Museum)*

Miniature mug, free-blown pale aquamarine glass. Height 1½ inches. New York State, c. 1800-1850. *(The Corning Museum of Glass)*

suring glasses. Tiny pitchers measure from 1½ inches to 2¾ inches in height. They are found with threaded neck and applied handles and feet. A rare pitcher with lily-pad decoration and crimped foot was made in South Jersey. Miniature pitchers were also made in

Miniature clear glass decanter; globular body, blown three-mold pattern; band of diamond diaper and sunburst motif between bands of vertical ribs; wheel stopper. Height 2⅜ inches. Boston and Sandwich Glass Company, 1826-1835. *(Courtesy Henry Francis du Pont Winterthur Museum)*

Miniature clear glass decanter. Blown three-mold pattern with band of diamond-diaper and sunburst motif between band of vertical ribs. Height 2¾ inches. Boston and Sandwich Glass Company, 1820-1850. *(Courtesy Henry Francis du Pont Winterthur Museum)*

blown three mold glass. These ranged in height, from 2 inches to 2¼ inches. They are found with geometric diamond patterns. The bodies were usually globular, shaped by manipulation, and the tiny looped handles had crimped ends. They were generally of clear glass but a rare dark sapphire pitcher blown in a toy decanter mold was made at Boston and Sandwich Glass Co. A miniature cruet was blown in a similar mold. Such hand-blown pieces are rare and no two are exactly alike while many such pieces may be "one of a kind." Miniature decanters, cordials and creamers are also found with sunburst

Two miniature decanters. LEFT: Decanter blown in full-sized mold in McKearin pattern G 11-19. New England, 1820-1835. Height 1⅜ inches. RIGHT: Free-blown decanter with applied spiral thread around neck. Height 4⁹⁄₁₆ inches. New England Glass Company, c. 1855. (*The Corning Museum of Glass*)

motifs and blocks of diamond diapering. Miniature pitchers and decanters according to McKearin* "are comparatively common in clear glass but in color are among the rarities." A rare dark sapphire blue pitcher and a canary decanter have been found. These Sandwich pieces may be the toy decanters advertised by the Boston and Sandwich Glass Company in 1825.

Miniature Lacy Glass was also made at Sandwich in the 1830's. There were tumblers, cups and saucers, covered bowls, compotes, plates, platters and pitchers. Cups and saucers were made in three styles in a flower pattern and in a rare shell design. Oval dishes in scroll design are found in clear, opal and opaque white. There

* McKearin, Helen & George S.: *American Glass,* Crown, 1948.

Group of American miniature glass. TOP LEFT: Clear blown pitcher. Height 2⅛ inches. TOP CENTER: Sugar bowl, early 19th Century. TOP RIGHT: Miniature glass pan, mid-19th Century. LOWER LEFT: Rare clear three-mold decanter in sunburst and diamond pattern. Height 2⅝ inches. Pitcher, sunburst and diamond pattern. Boston and Sandwich Glass Company. Plate, lacy pressed, blue with stippled ground and floral border. Lacy oval dish, clear, honeysuckle and scroll design. Sandwich. Candlestick, hexagonal stem, yellow green, two-mold, late 19th Century. (*Courtesy of The Henry Ford Museum, Dearborn, Michigan*)

LEFT: Two blown three-mold miniature pitchers, diamond sunburst between ribbing. Height 2⅛ inches. RIGHT: Blown three-mold pitcher with diamond sunburst between ribbing. Height 2⅜ inches. Boston and Sandwich Glass Company. (*Taylor & Dull photo*)

Miniature pitcher with witch ball stopper; free-blown pale aquamarine glass with lily pad decoration. Height 2½ inches. c. 1800-1850. South Jersey. (*The Corning Museum of Glass*)

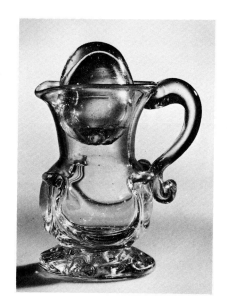

are also rare footed octagonal bowls and bowls in Gothic Arch pattern, Honeycomb and conventional patterns with stipple flowers in panel or scalloped edges. Miniature covered dishes or compotes were not made in the exact designs of large dishes. In size they range from 1⅝ inches by 1½ inches to 2⅞ inches by 2⅞. They are found in opaque amethyst, yellow, opal, blue and clear glass. Tiny tumblers

Miniature washbowl and pitcher, dark green glass pressed in lacy pattern. Height overall 3 inches. Boston and Sandwich Glass Company, c. 1830-1845. *(The Corning Museum of Glass)*

Miniature clear glass basket; blown three-mold with vertical ribbing, horizontal rib band and diamond diapering. Height 2¾ inches. American, 1820-1850. *(Courtesy Henry Francis du Pont Winterthur Museum)*

LEFT: Toy condiment set on tray. Milk Glass; RIGHT: Toy sugar and creamer. Late 19th Century. *(Westmoreland Glass Company)*

1½ inches by 1⅜ have a design of diamond points with a star at the base. They are found in crystal and rare sapphire blue. Toy creamers, 1½ inches high, have a scalloped or plain foot with a rosette handle.

Miniature vegetable dishes ⁹⁄₁₆ of an inch high, which may have been part of a set, are found with diamond and scroll pattern with two hearts on the bottom. Other tiny dishes have a scroll and flower pattern on a stippled ground. Pitchers and matching bowls were made in basket-of-flower design and other lacy patterns. Miniature American glass was also made in later pressed glass patterns including Cable, Saw-tooth, Honeycomb, Waffle, Swirl, Hobnail, Cube, and Grape. Tiny creamers measure 2 inches in height. A four-piece miniature set was made in Liberty Bell and a creamer, sugar bowl, butter dish and spoon holder in Lion pattern.

In the mid-1900's the Westmoreland Glass Company of Grapeville, Pennsylvania, made a group of crystal pressed glass miniatures. These were made as toys for children. The pieces included a toy water set consisting of a pitcher and six tumblers; a berry set of seven pieces including a bowl and six sauce dishes; a punch set con-

Toy punch set pressed in pattern imitating cut glass. Height of bowl 4½ inches; cups 2 inches. Mid-19th Century. (*Westmoreland Glass Company*)

Toy pressed water set. Height of pitcher, 3¾ inches; tumblers, 2 inches. Mid-19th Century. *(Westmoreland Glass Company)*

Group of glass miniatures. Lacy table wares and iron. Boston and Sandwich Glass Company, 1830-1850. Bottle and candlesticks. Height 1¾ inches to 2¹¹⁄₁₆ inches. *(The Corning Museum of Glass)*

sisting of a footed punch bowl and six cups; a four-piece toy set in-cluding a spoon holder. These sets continued to be made as late as 1927 and are included in the company price list of that date. There were also sets made in Milk Glass including a condiment set and a jelly, sugar and cream set which is still made today.

In the 1880's sets of toy hobnail glass were made by Adams & Company of Pittsburgh. Miniature Ruby-Stained pattern glass was also made in several patterns. Several styles of miniature creamers and sugars were made in Ruby Thumbprint. The creamers are about 3 inches high and the sugars were also made in Arched Ovals, Pan-eled English, Hobnail with Prisms, Late Block, Button Arches and Rib & Button by the various Pittsburgh and other Pennsylvania glass companies. Ruby-stained glass was a late Victorian novelty.

Miniature cut glass was also made. There were miniature punch bowls and cups with fine cutting. There were also miniatures made as novelties such as the Gone-with-the-Wind lamp which was made in emerald green cut to clear and has a sterling silver base. Small dishes, pitchers and ice buckets were made as salesmen's sam-ples. Tiny books were made to be used as paperweights and small hearts, diamonds, spades and clubs were sold in a set to be used as bridge prizes. Cut glass was made by Bakewell as early as 1808. The New England Glass Company and the Boston and Sandwich Company also made early cut glass. American companies who made later cut glass were John L. Gilliland of New York; Dorflinger Green-point Glass Works, Brooklyn; Thomas G. Hawkes of Corning, New York, and such later companies as Libbey, Sinclaire and Tuthill. But about 1900 cheap imitations were made and these continued to be made into the twentieth century. Several types of miniature vases have been found in rare Purple Slag or Marble Glass.

Miniature glass lamps were among the first items made at Sandwich c. 1825. In the late nineteenth century tiny miniature lamps were made in the various types of glass then popular, including clear and colored glass, Milk Glass, Satin Glass, Spangled Glass and art glass such as Tiffany Favrile. Many of the lamps were small models of larger lamps, including metal student lamps. Others were

Miniature glass lamps. TOP ROW: Left, Spatter glass, light green, 9½ inches high. Right, opaque glass with Maltese cross and swag and tassel, 9½ inches high. CENTER ROW: Green glass with raised leaves and gold decoration. Right, same lamp in amethyst. CENTER: Artichoke lamp in rose and green. BOTTOM ROW: Left to right, opaque white with molded decoration; blue polka dot satin glass with bulb shade; pink satin glass with diamond quilt and puffed pattern. *(Collection of Mrs. Edward J. Delmore)*

Miniature lamps. TOP ROW: Delphinium blue transparent glass with globe shade and clusters of flowers in relief. Height 7½ inches. Brass student lamp with opalescent white shade. Height 12 inches. Opaque blue lamp with sawtooth and prism pattern. Height 6 inches. MIDDLE ROW: Molded shell, acanthus, and flower decoration on

opaque glass. Height 7½ inches. Forest green satin finish glass decorated in enamel cyclamen buds and leaves. Height 8½ inches. Green transparent glass lamp decorated in flowers and dots. Height 7½ inches. Stippled rosette with squatty base and globe shade, transparent camphor finish in orange red. BOTTOM ROW: Blue polka dot satin glass lamp with square crimped shade. Height 8 inches. Tulip lamp, red satin finish, bronze base. Pink Diamond quilted and puffed cased glass. Height 8 inches. Opaque lavender, pink and sea-green with molded spiral pattern and acanthus leaves. (*Collection of Mrs. Edward J. Delmore*)

made in novelty shapes such as animal, bird and human forms. These include a reclining elephant, an owl, a swan, a St. Nicholas and a log cabin or schoolhouse. These Victorian novelty lamps were in great demand when made and are also popular with collectors today and are now becoming scarce and expensive.

TIFFANY

TIFFANY Favrile glass which is so popular with collectors today was first exhibited in 1894. It continued to be made until 1920. Tiffany, like the rest of the world of the late nineteenth century, was interested in the excavations of ancient glass objects in the Middle East. He was fascinated by the shapes and especially by the iridescence of these objects which had developed after centuries of lying buried in the earth. Favrile glass is the result of Tiffany's study of this antique glass and his own experimentation. He reversed the process of the natural decay of glass and thus obtained his iridescent and luster effects.

Favrile glass is a composition of various colored glasses worked together while hot. A piece began with an iridescent ball of glass from the furnace. The workman charged it at certain pre-arranged points with textures and different colors. The ball was then returned to the fire and again the process was repeated, sometimes as many as twenty times. When all the different glasses had been combined and manipulated and the desired form and size attained the ornament too blended into a pre-arranged design. The metallic luster was produced by exposing a metal film to vapors or gases. Gold chloride was used in suspension in the glass and also sprayed on the hot surface, the latter creating the satin-like texture. The lustrous patina and richness was described by Tiffany in his patent application of 1880. "The effect is a highly iridescent one and of pleasing

LEFT: Paneled urn-shaped vessel with formalized yellow and green leaf. Label, Tiffany-Favrile. Height 1⅝ inches. RIGHT: Olive green and yellow miniature vase. Squat short-necked, patterned with spiral leaflike stripes of deep yellow and gray-green interspersed with dots.

LEFT: Squat blue and black miniature vase with crimps at sides. Decorated with spiral striated leaves in blue and silver iridescence on black ground. Height 2 inches. Inscribed "X 2756" with label. CENTER: Brown and white miniature vase. RIGHT: Ovate brown vase with iridescent collar of leaf-like motifs. Height 3¾ inches. Inscribed "L. C. Tiffany Favrile V376." *(Taylor & Dull photo)*

LEFT: Miniature ovoid vase with ochre stripes on gray-green. Inscribed "L.C.T. R 341." Height 2 inches. RIGHT: Ovoid vase marbled green and ochre with loops and swirls in olive green, brown and ochre. Inscribed "L.C.T. D. 210." Height 2¾ inches. *(Taylor & Dull photo)*

LEFT: Blue bottle-form vase decorated with vertical serrated stripes. Height 3¾ inches, with label. CENTER: Short-necked spherical vase with pattern of spiraling vertebrate stripes in blue and ivory on amber ground with iridescence. Inscribed "L.C.T. 09965" with label. Height 2¼ inches. RIGHT: Conical form vase with brown and ochre stripes. Inscribed "L. C. Tiffany-Favrile, R 239." Height 3⅛ inches. *(Taylor & Dull photo)*

LEFT: Ovoid miniature vase with flaring foot. White decorated with green vines. Inscribed "L.C.T. Favrile 3948 P." Height 1⅞ inches. RIGHT: Brown and white vase with handles and collar of brown and yellow leaves. Tiffany Favrile. Height 2⅞ inches. (*Taylor & Dull photo*)

metallic luster, changeable from one to the other, depending upon the direction of the visual ray and the brilliancy or dullness of the light falling upon or passing through the glass." Tiffany adapted shapes for his designs in glass from ancient Middle Eastern, Iberian and Islamic forms. He was also influenced by the Far East and by Chinese and Japanese forms and designs. He avoided harsh color and over-elaboration in his designs. His favorite motifs were the peacock feather and waves. He also delighted in natural forms—the veinings of leaves, flower stems, lily pads and separate petals as well as the whole blossom. The designs and colors are fluid but always cling to the shape of the vase. The colors range from clear crystal through the rainbow to a deep opaque black and there were thousands of different shades and varieties of glass. Greens, blues, and golds blend in iridescent beauty as in a natural peacock feather. There are also opaque blues and vases with red overlay on a black or green ground or gold threads overlaid on a marbleized green ground. Tiffany also used other complex techniques, including the mille fiori or paperweight technique, and there are vases with mille fiori leaves and flowers. Two types of vases take their forms and techniques from excavated pieces, namely the iridescent volcano or Lava Ware vases with their squashed irregular shapes and the pitted iridescent cypriote wares.

Although Tiffany's approach was traditional and he took much from the past he also advocated the use of new and unconventional forms and techniques.

Tiffany miniature or cabinet pieces followed similar forms, designs, colors and techniques of those of the larger pieces although

LEFT: Miniature ribbed form vase, yellow with gold iridescence. Height 1¹⁵⁄₁₆ inches. Quezal Art Glass and Decorating Co., Brooklyn, N.Y. 1902-1920. CENTER: Amber vase with ribbed and twisted neck and blue-green iridescence. Height 5¹⁄₁₆ inches. Tiffany Glass Works, N.Y. RIGHT: Miniature violet vase with blue iridescence. Height 3¼ inches. Quezal Art Glass & Decorating Co. (*The Toledo Museum of Art*)

they are never copies. Each tiny vase was an individual creation and there were no two alike. The great variety makes any classification of shapes or styles very difficult. Tiffany miniature vases were of antique amphora shape, spherical and trumpet-shaped. However, bulbous, pear, and gourd shapes predominated although many miniatures are squat urn or ovoid-shaped. Many other forms were irregular and inventive and uniquely his own. Combed and marbleized combinations in a variety of colors and flowing lines were the predominant ornamentation but overlay and mille fiori and carved cameo techniques were also frequently used.

Descriptions of Tiffany miniatures not only give an idea of the beauty of the coloring but also indicate the excellence of the glassblower's art. Indeed these small masterpieces far excel the beauty of many larger pieces as they also excel in price. There are tiny vases of iridescent blue and gold; gold vases with white paperweight flowers, green leaves and vines; white vases with gold swirls and green vases with silver swirls; gold vases with green mille fiori; gold iridescent vases with green leaves and vines; blue vines and leaves on black; green vases with orange vines and flowers and rare black miniatures with swirls of silver and lavender. A squat red miniature 1⅜ inches with a collar of silver loop design and silver swirls at the base is marked "L.C.T.P." A squat urn-shaped iridescent blue vessel 2¾ inches high is decorated with iridescent leaf fronds. It is inscribed "Louis C. Tiffany 03242." Miniature Tiffany Favrile cabinet pieces range in size from 1¼ inches to 4¼ inches in height. Larger pieces are usually not classed as miniatures.

The earliest pieces were not for sale and were not signed. Those which were numbered also have a "X" and later pieces not meant for sale were marked with an "X." A paper label was affixed to the base. The pieces first offered for sale had two paper labels, one with the monogram of the Tiffany Glass and Decorating Company and one with the registry number. Many early pieces, however, are without marks but these are rare. A rare early mark is inscribed "T.G.C." (Tiffany Glass Co.). This is found on a black iridescent miniature 2½ inches high with blue iridescent vines and leaves. When the numbering system was established each individual piece was marked with the Tiffany name or initials and all unusual pieces with a number and a letter of the alphabet. Those with prefix letters A to N were made from 1896 to 1900, those with P to Z from 1901 to 1905. Those with A to N after the number date from 1905 to 1912 and those with P to Z from 1913 to 1920 when production was discontinued. The letter O before the number meant a special order. Some of these latter pieces were made for exhibition and were not for sale. Those which Tiffany especially liked and wanted to keep for his own collection were signed with his own hand and marked "A-Coll."

Tiffany had many imitators and competitors both in Europe and at home in America. Most of their products lacked the imagination and inventive design of Tiffany Favrile. Martin Bach, Sr. and William Overend, who had been among Tiffany's glass workers, set up the Quezal Art Glass and Decorating Company in Brooklyn in 1902. Their Quezal glass was of green, crimson and gold on white, gold and green grounds. Modern leaf patterns have iridescent gold spots. Victor Durand, another Tiffany craftsman, joined the Vineland Glass Works at Vineland, New Jersey, and marketed a Tiffany-type iridescent glass under the name of Durand Art Glass. Many of these vases had scroll designs in blue and orange. At Somerville, Massa-

Tiffany miniature white with platinum and green iridescent decoration. Height 2 inches; width 1½ inches. Signed and numbered. *(Courtesy Sharp's 1860 Antiques)*

chusetts, the Union Glass Works marketed an iridescent glass under the name of Kew Blas.

The most successful competitor of Tiffany was Frederick Carder, an Englishman. Carder formed the Steuben Glass Works in Corning, New York, and made superior iridescent glass called Aurene. Aurene was made in classic shapes with naturalistic designs covered with an iridescent coating. The colors ranged from gold, light greens and blues to brilliant peacock colorings. Aurene, like Tiffany's Favrile, is individually fashioned.

ART GLASS

DIMINUTIVE examples of skilled glassmaking are to be found in almost every technique and in every category of glass from hand-blown to the various types of art glass of the late nineteenth century. Amberina glass was made at the New England Glass Company in the 1880's and 1890's. It was also made at Mount Washington and it is difficult to distinguish pieces made at one factory from those made at the other. The glass is pale amber shading to rich ruby. It was made in table and ornamental wares and was also made in miniature vases and creamers. These range in size from 2 inches to 3¼ inches in height. The handles on the creamers are clear and some have applied rick-rack decoration. Some pieces were patterned in molds of expanded diamond or ogival design or inverted Thumbprint and ribbing. A miniature gold Aurene Jack-in-the-Pulpit vase is 4½ inches high and is signed "Aurene no. 137."

Pomona glass was also produced at the New England Glass Company. It was a blown clear glass treated with etching or staining of pale red to amber. Tiny pitchers and bowls were made in Pomona glass. There are also rare miniatures of Burmese glass with both dull and glossy finish and colors shading from greenish yellow to delicate pink. Satin glass miniatures were made in plain delicate colors of blue, green, yellow, orange and deep pink. Satin glass was also made in patterns of diamond quilt, herringbone, polka dot and swirls. Tiny

TOP LEFT: Early overlay creamer, cobalt blue cut to white. Height 2½ inches. TOP CENTER: New England Amberina creamer with applied "rick-rack" decoration. c. 1883. Height 3¼ inches. TOP RIGHT: Webb Peachblow vase. Soft rose shading to deep rose, ivory lining, satin finish. Height 2¾ inches. LOWER LEFT: Amberina pitcher shading amber to cranberry, clear applied handle. Height 2¼ inches. LOWER CENTER: Miniature vase with inverted thumbprint design. Amber shading to ruby, blue at top. Height 3 inches. LOWER RIGHT: New England Amberina creamer. Height 2¼ inches. *(Maude B. Feld)*

pitchers, rose bowls and perfume bottles are available. There were also small pitchers and mugs of Mary Gregory design that were made as cabinet pieces. These had typical scenes of children and flowers painted in white on backgrounds of blue or rose glass.

Cameo glass, which dates from Roman times, became popular in the mid-eighteenth century after the discovery of the famous Portland Vase. Reproductions of this vase were exhibited by John Northwood at the 1851 exposition in London. There were other English makers of Cameo glass. John, Thomas and George Woodall (1850-1925) were well-known makers of Cameo glass and the firm of Thomas Webb & Sons made quantities of Cameo glass. Webb made many miniature pieces. The cut designs are of flowers and leaves in

TOP LEFT: Miniature rose bowl, rainbow Satin glass with pattern of diamond quilting. Height c. 2 inches. TOP RIGHT: Miniature Spangled Glass basket with twisted over-shot handles. Height c. 3 inches. BOTTOM ROW: Three miniature Spangled Glass baskets with twisted over-shot handles. (*The Bennington Museum*)

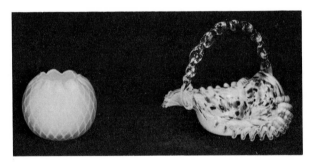

red and white, yellow and white, brown and white and other color combinations. Cameo glass was made by dipping the dark opaque glass into a white vitreous opaque mixture and the designs were then carved. Cameo glass miniatures were also made in America at Mt. Washington Glass Company, Boston and Sandwich Glass Company, New England Glass Company, Bakewell, Pears and Company and Atterbury Company in the late 1880's.

In about 1910 a method of giving pressed glass an iridized

New England Pomona, square-mouth creamer, red to amber. Height 3 inches. (*Maude B. Feld*)

Miniature Cameo Glass vase. Floral in high relief on red background. Height c. 3½ inches. English, mid-19th Century. (*Courtesy Sharp's 1860 Antiques*)

finish produced quantities of low cost iridescent wares. This cheap iridescent glass was first made by the Harry Northwood Company of Wheeling, West Virginia. It is known as Carnival or Taffeta glass and was made by many companies until the 1920's. Carnival glass was made in many colors, including marigold, cobalt blue, amethyst, purple, green and rare red. The pressed patterns include flowers, fruit, birds including the peacock, animals and conventional cut glass motifs. More than fourteen hundred patterns have been identified. However, what concerns us here is the miniature. A water set consisting of a small water pitcher and tumblers made in marigold is miniature size.

INDEX

179